Interpretation, Deconstruction, and Ideology

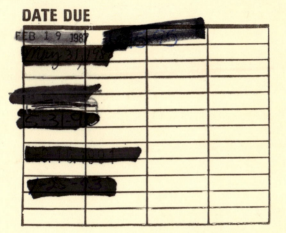

Interpretation, Deconstruction, and Ideology

AN INTRODUCTION TO SOME CURRENT ISSUES IN LITERARY THEORY

CHRISTOPHER BUTLER

CLARENDON PRESS · OXFORD

1984

Oxford University Press, Walton Street, Oxford OX2 6DP

London New York Toronto
Delhi Bombay Calcutta Madras Karachi
Kuala Lumpur Singapore Hong Kong Tokyo
Nairobi Dar es Salaam Cape Town
Melbourne Auckland

and associates in
Beirut Berlin Ibadan Mexico City Nicosia

Oxford is a trade mark of Oxford University Press

Published in the United States
by Oxford University Press, New York

British Library Cataloguing in Publication Data

Butler, Christopher, 1940–
Interpretation, deconstruction, and ideology.
1. literature——Philosophy
I. Title
801   PN45

ISBN 0–19–815792–4
ISBN 0–19–815791–6 Pbk

Set by Set Fair Limited, London
Printed in Great Britain by the Thetford Press Limited, Thetford, Norfolk

For
my mother,
and to the memory of
my father

Contents

Introduction

The student of literature is at present confronted by a bewildering variety of theoretical positions and vocabularies. Many teachers believe the subject has entered into a state of crisis, which has been sustained since the advent of structuralism by the rise of deconstructive analyses of literature. I wish to ask in what follows how far new theoretical models for criticism reflect the type of intellectual upheaval which occurs when the paradigms for common practices change, and how far the shifts of methodological allegiance amongst teachers and students may be directed to further pragmatic ends. I interrelate and criticize linguistic, structuralist, deconstructive and Marxist approaches to the text, which have previously tended to be discussed separately.

I thus wish to take the reader through some of the most important theoretical issues that he will have to confront along with the individual text. These are the ways in which it is made intelligible in reading, its relationship to linguistic description, its (possible) reference to the external world, its susceptibility to deconstructive analysis, and finally its relationship to frameworks of belief or ideology which the interpreter may himself wish to promote. I approach these problematic areas by analysing what I take to be the underlying logic of typical examples of the interpretative strategy at issue.

In doing so I of course attempt to argue for a coherent position of my own, which encompasses what we might reasonably say when we interpret a text. I therefore begin by investigating the way in which it may have implications—our theory of meaning. This will reflect a balance between our understanding of 'what the text means' and what we may want to say in declaring that meaning, our making of interpretations. These do not simply reflect our understanding, for in so far as they are passed on to an audience they have pragmatic purposes.

As I hope will emerge in what follows, I mean by this pragmatist approach to interpretation to develop a theory which is not concerned with the pursuit of the ultimate 'truth' about the text : this is because most texts can be seen to be radically ambiguous, and cast in a language that is incapable of giving us a consistent picture of reality, which the interpreter can pass on. The languages available for interpretation are also plural, and they too cannot be cast into a single consistent overriding system. In this situation we must ask not, 'Is my interpretation true?' but more self-consciously perhaps, 'What language for interpretation am I using, and for what purposes?' Once aware of such purposes, we may be better able to chose between interpretative methods.

For if the text has multiple implications amongst which the interpreter chooses, and if the interpreter can also choose amongst structuralist, deconstructionist, Marxist, and liberal moralist frameworks for interpretation, then the apparent anarchy of pluralism can at least be brought into some order, and lose its air of indifferentism, if we ask that within the theory of interpretation interpreters should be as clear as possible about the ends for which they interpret. For example, we may attempt to show how aporias and contradictions arise within any 'logocentric' or 'realist' approach to language, or to show the way in which apparently individualist characterization is caught up within a larger social process of class conflict. Such interpretations, I argue, use the text not only to help us think the right things as we read it, but also to get us to accept intellectual norms of further consequence—in the cases cited, those of scepticism or of the Marxist analysis of historical development. It is not some notion of truth to the meaning of the text (though I shall argue in my opening chapters that this can be more clearly defined), but pragmatic ends that are important within the theory of interpretation. This is because such a theory must attempt to do justice to the fact that within institutions like universities which support interpretative activity, there are competing intellectual frameworks which appeal to and attempt to enclose different interpretative communities.

In what follows I do not attempt to reconcile these competing groups, since I believe that there is no metasystem for interpretation that would make such a reconciliation possible. I attempt rather to clarify for the reader who may be bewildered by this conflict various interpretative procedures, and the ends to which he or she might be committed in adopting them. To this extent I attempt to produce a pragmatic theory of interpretation.

In writing this book I have incurred a number of debts, to the Governing Body of Christ Church for leave, to my students for their questioning attitudes, to my wife for her generous and continuing support, and more particularly to Thomas Docherty, Terry Eagleton, and Ian Maclean for their detailed comments. None of these are of course responsible for the faults that remain.

1 Implication

The interpretation of a text typically goes beyond what it simply seems to say, and brings out in various ways its implications. This concern for implication is essential to our understanding of all types of linguistic usage, including the most simple. Indeed those texts which we conventionally treat as 'literary' are not particularly distinctive in having implicit meaning, for so also do newspaper reports, philosophical essays, lovers' quarrels, speeches by American Presidents, and accounts of dreams as given to psychoanalysts.

I wish to argue further that in all such cases, what it is reasonable to say about these implications ultimately depends upon what we take to be the situation referred to in conversation or projected by a text. The presupposition here is that language is a system which can make satisfactory representations of 'reality'. I thus begin by presenting a mimetic view of interpretation; one which as we shall later see, is persuasively challenged by many contemporary critical theorists. According to this view, the meaning of sentences, and above them of discourses and texts, has to be interpreted in context, as relevant to a situation, which thereby activates a complex of beliefs in the speaker and hearer or author and reader. And they are interpretable in so far as they can be shown to observe a number of principles which underly all communicative exchanges.[1]

On this model, utterances and sentences in texts will have a range of implications which the interpreter may have to specify. Some of these implications may be described as logically derived, in the sense that we would want to say that anyone who had a mature command of the language involved would have to accept at least these implications. Thus to use Smith and Wilson's example, the sentence, 'My son threw a brick at the window' has a number of entailments to which the speaker would have to be committed, such as, 'I have a child', 'My child threw a brick at something', and so on.[2] From this point of view, a sentence may be taken to mean by implication a set of propositions which represent its semantic structure: its semantic entailments. The relative firmness of this structure will be important for the interpretation of metaphor.

To these logical entailments we nearly always have to add the contextual determinants of implicit meaning. These perform the immensely important task of helping us to see how one part of a conversation or text may be relevant to another. Thus Smith and

Wilson give the example of a discussion concerning two contenders for the Nobel Prize : it is presupposed that only one writer can win it at a time, and that two writers, Patrick White and Barbara Cartland, are in contention. Thus if one of the speakers remarks 'Well, it won't be Patrick White', he contextually implies that Barbara Cartland will win the Nobel Prize.[3]

This kind of pragmatic implication is only plausible within a particular context of knowledge and belief, shared between the sender of the text and its receiver. Thus our model for interpretation must include not only a body of linguistic knowledge (a grammar) but also a background of knowledge and belief (an 'encyclopaedia' for short) which can if necessary be made explicit in interpretation.

These taken together are the basis for the pragmatic logic, or series of conventions, which underly speaker/hearer and author/text/reader relationships. On these assumptions texts, like conversations, will have a large body of unstated meanings which interpretation, in so far as it makes the text explicit, will have to reveal. The question then arises: could there be a rational (and thus fairly certain) mode of proceeding in this area? How do we combine the logic, the 'encyclopaedia', and the pragmatic conventions implied by the text in such a way as to allow us to see how one part of the text is relevant to another, and so release this further information? For texts often enough have gaps and breaks which the reader–critic has to fill in in order to make the language before him intelligible.

Such pragmatic implications can be less straightforward than they were in the Nobel Prize example, as we can see from the following rather Pinteresque exchange :

A: Your son's really taken to Annette.
B: He used to like playing with snails when he was a child.

On the assumption that B's remark was intended as relevant, the hearer must set about finding the relevant pragmatic implication. Now nothing directly follows from A and B together that does not follow from either in isolation; moreover, on fairly normal assumptions about background knowledge, there will be no item of shared knowledge which can be used as an additional premise establishing a connection between A and B. What is to be done? A hearer who persists in regarding B as relevant might reason as follows. B's remark was intended to be relevant. Therefore there must be some additional premise I could use to derive relevant information from A and B together. Since I know of none, I'll have to construct one. He might construct one as follows. B's remark suggests that his son has strange tastes. If liking Annette was also a strange taste, then B's remark would carry a further implication : a normal person would not like Annette. Therefore there must be something wrong with Annette. The final result of this reasoning is a pragmatic implication derived from A and B together, and thus establishing the relevance of B's remark. Of course this is not the only possible interpretation, but most are along similar lines . . . What is important is that the hearer has to supply additional premises of his own, premises in which he does not necessarily believe, yielding pragmatic implications which he also need not necessarily believe.[4]

Pragmatic implications of this type are the staple of interpretation. The general assumption they involve is of the type 'A was meant to be relevant to B', or more impersonally in the case of the literary text, 'in the cultural surroundings of this text, A can plausibly be shown as being relevant to B'. The mode of its relevance can be shown in interpretation : in the above instance, by a strategy we will find to be important in metaphor, that of locating the unstated common denominator : 'having strange tastes'. Of course we have not got very far in demonstrating this by citing a linguist's example of a scrap of conversation. But even on this level, consider the vast implications, with all their reference back to the past of the plot which provides their context, of an exchange between Adam Verver and Maggie at the end of *The Golden Bowl*. Adam, we remember, has an 'intention of leaving his wife to her devices' once he has renounced London, and its artistic treasures, and we expect Maggie and her Prince to be reconciled. They are both looking at a picture, an 'early Florentine sacred subject'. Father says to daughter : 'It's all right, eh?'; and she replies 'Oh my dear—rather!' The interpretative significance of all this is reinforced by James's subsequent intervention to urge the reader to recontextualize the implications of what they have said: 'He had applied the question to the great fact of the picture, as she had spoken for the picture in reply, but it was as if these words for an instant afterwards symbolised another truth, so that they looked about at everything else to give them another extension.'[5] Of course we have to do this 'looking about' and James exploits such implications with relentless virtuosity. For example, if we are attentive to the thematic structure of the novel, we will probably remember how often the Prince himself has been spoken of as a work of art which Adam has bought for his daughter.

As the James example shows, our ability to attribute the correct implication to what characters say may depend upon our growing knowledge within the text of what we take to be their personal history. This is a crucial element in a novel like Claude Mauriac's *Le Dîner en ville* (1959) in which the guests at a dinner party all converse without having their remarks attributed to them in the text and the reader is challenged (by building up a picture of the speaker's character and what he or she is likely to say) to learn how to attribute the remarks reported in the text to their correct speakers.

The implications of conversations within texts are thus highly controlled by the contextual knowledge supplied by the reader; and literary works are more or less 'difficult' in this respect, from the essentially dialogue form of the novels of Ivy Compton-Burnett, through the sudden twists of topic in Pinter's plays, to the often irredeemably ambiguous and indeterminable dialogue of Donald Barthelme's *Great Days* collection, in which the pragmatic implications of the speakers' remarks are perpetually as indirect as in the 'Annette' exchange, and often seem to be in conflict, so that no consistent interpretation can be given.

However, my aim at this point is not to interpret particular texts; it is to point to some of the complexities for interpretation of the obvious fact that such exchanges have a context of situation which may activate relevant knowledge and belief and consequently give us grounds for seeing one part of a text as relevant to another.[6] I now wish to show that similar considerations apply to our understanding of any non-fictional or fictional text, whether conversation is involved or not; the chief difference being that the (literary) text, unlike everyday conversation, often has to create its own context of situation, which I shall call, following Halliday, the 'co-text'. For the text is typically 'internally cohesive, and it functions as a whole as the relevant environment for the operation of the theme and information systems'.[7] By the latter, Halliday means the text's own topics and what is said about them. I shall in what follows attempt to distinguish between co-text in this sense and 'context', by which I shall mean the situation of the text in the world. This will include such matters as the text's referring 'beyond itself' to 'external reality'.

The passage I am about to cite will show that we look for interpretative implications even in the reading of the sort of simple prose to which no one would think of attaching an interpretation of the complicated kind habitual to literary critics.[8] I have numbered the sentences to facilitate my own commentary:

(1) Business had been slow since the oil crisis.

(2) Nobody seemed to want anything really elegant anymore.

(3) Suddenly the door opened and a well-dressed man entered the showroom.

(4) John put on his friendliest and most sincere expression and walked toward the man.

As is made clear in Rumelhart's analysis of this passage, most readers, in trying to construct a coherent situation for it, see that it implies far more than it states, and these implications can be brought to consciousness in a slow-motion account of our reading. For 'as the sentences are read, schemata are activated, evaluated, refined or discarded', and various readers' interpretations of their relevance to one another are remarkably consistent.[9] Their basic aim is to make the passage coherent, by seeing how one sentence follows from another (though not necessarily in any strictly logical sense of entailment). The interpretation of each sentence is also made relative to the interpretation of its successors. Thus (1) expresses a belief on the part of the speaker/writer, and by reference to our knowledge of the world, we can infer a causal relationship within it—business is slow *because* of the oil crisis. Therefore the business involved must be dependent in some way upon oil, and further may involve selling cars or petrol. But if we take (2) as relevant to (1) on the principles outlined above, we find that the petrol hypothesis is squashed by the word 'elegant' in (2), and so the car hypothesis is likely to win : it is quickly confirmed by the reference to 'showroom' in (3). We thus make explicit the implied relationships between (1–3) by scanning back and forth between them, and inferring that the business is that of selling cars and that 'elegant' cars are likely to be difficult to sell, when we remember that they are of kind to consume a lot of petrol. This inference arises from the background premiss supplied by the reader, that oil crises cause rises in petrol prices, and that these rises may deter people from buying cars that are expensive to run. This clumsy exposition of what the reader takes in at a glance goes some way to confirm van Dijk's assertion that 'Natural discourse, unlike formal discourse [as in mathematics or formal logic] is not fully explicit. Relationships between sentences and propositions may exist without being expressed. This is why the theoretical construct of a text is necessary to show how discourses can be coherently interpreted even if most of the propositions necessary to establish coherence remain implicit.'[10]

Similar inferences structure the rest of the passage. The 'well-dressed' man further combines with 'anything very elegant' to suggest a particularly expensive kind of car, on the implicit, and stereotypical assumption that well-dressed men are probably rich. With all this in mind we can identify 'John' as likely to be a salesman, particularly as his actions are also stereotypical. His expression is designed, we assume, to help him make a good impression in making a sale. We interpret (4) as caused by (3).[11] Now much of the information we have brought to bear is not explicitly stated in the passage at all—John is a car salesman, probably fallen on hard times, the type of car he is likely to sell is expensive, well-dressed men are good prospects for a sale, his expression is a sign that he wishes to make one, and so on. All the inferences are derived from our seeing all four sentences as having a relevance to one another by implications which are mediated by our construction of a coherent fictional situation, the co-text.

I referred earlier to the reader's use of basic schemata, which enable him to frame hypotheses and to discern the implicative relationships between sentences. These frames or schemata are basic to our understanding. It is difficult to fix on an exact terminology in this area. Van Dijk defines a frame as 'the set of propositions characterising our conventional knowledge of some more or less autonomous situation/activity/course of events/state.'[12] Beaugrande suggests that we reserve 'frame' for the mental network of elements we bring to the text (arranged around a 'control centre', as when we think, say, of the parts of a *house*), and 'schema' for our ordered use of these elements in comprehending texts.[13] I will attempt to follow this distinction between frame (background knowledge) and schema (the ordered use of it) in what follows.

Within the frame then (that, say, of 'selling goods'), certain types of action and setting are rational or likely, and our schema-processing of the text will confirm or disconfirm the expectations which the frame sets up. All texts are in a reciprocal relationship with such frames and schemata, which are the higher order mental counterparts of our 'social semiotics' or 'meaning systems within the culture', as Halliday describes them.[14] The exact status for interpretation of these frames is a matter of considerable interest and dispute. I am inclined to agree with van Dijk that they are theoretical primitives.[15] They reflect a part of our knowledge of the world as it is encoded within the conceptual structure of our semantic memory. They are our basic or organizing principles for understanding and relating concepts which by convention and experience are felt to form a 'unity'.

This relationship may always be challenged, and typically is by literary works. Our sense of conceptual unity may ultimately depend upon the way we believe things are in the world : thus in the case of 'He went to the beach and Peter was born in Manchester', we do not feel that the sentence is connected, because we fail to discern 'a relation between the facts denoted by its clauses'.[16] We will discuss this unifying function of the frame in greater detail when we look at metaphors and the role of semantic fields in poetic structure (2 and 3.1). Once a text activates such a frame, we become aware of those elements which typically belong together within it. Think, for example of what we might expect in reading about someone entering a restaurant—or a church. We may then find that Larkin's 'Church Going' is in fact a schematic subversion of such a typical framework. Of course it is almost impossible in this area to distinguish between 'linguistic' and 'factual' knowledge, for example in the interrelationship between our command of the lexicon of language, and our stock of beliefs about the world.

However, if the notions of frame and schema are accepted, we can see that 'the interpretation of sentences would no longer be relative only to the sequence of previous sentences of a discourse, but also relative to the set of propositions of a particular frame.'[17] At its largest, this set of propositions comprises our most general beliefs about the world, which we bring to the beginning of the text, and which may have to be discarded for the purposes of the text (if for example we are reading fantasy literature). In reading, our contextual conception of the world and the text's own projection inevitably confront one another. We must see the text, at least initially, as mimetic, since our knowledge of the meaning of its expressions is so largely drawn from experience, though the potential dangers of sustaining this response through to the end will be discussed in full later.[18]

One might note that essentially the same process of comprehension would be involved, whether the passage we are concerned with is taken to be factual and historical or fictional. There do however seem to be fictional 'markers' in passages like that we cited from Rumelhart. For example the use of a past narrative tense, the switch to narrative present with 'suddenly' which dramatizes the passage, and the use of a quasi-omniscient comment, 'Nobody . . .' which makes a claim typical of fiction, to know the unexpressed attitudes of a character. This carries also, I think, the implication that 'really elegant' is John's type of formulation. This oscillation between what the observing narrator might report and what his characters might think, is carried through to 'his friendliest and most sincere smile', which is ambiguously poised, with its intentional verb, 'put on' : would John think, or admit, that he was doing this? The last two sentences thus make of the first two a possible implicit reflection of the character John, rather than of the narrator; and so on.

All this suggests very strongly that our awareness of fiction is a cognitive one. We consider the likelihood of the information we have as being conveyed historically, from the point of view of an external observer presenting factual evidence, or as invoking the typically non-historical procedures of fiction (an omniscient tense structure; a tendency to report thoughts and actions as if one had privileged access to other people's minds, and so on). This dialectic between the apparent historical accuracy of the text and those literary conventions which may be taken to subvert or support it is, as we shall see, central to interpretation.

2.1 Metaphor in the Text

> I bridle in my struggling Muse with Pain
> That longs to launch into a nobler strain.
> To *bridle a goddess* is no very delicate idea; but why must she be bridled?
> because she *longs to launch*, an act which was never hindered by a *bridle* : and
> whither will she launch? Into a *nobler strain*. She is in the first line a horse, in
> the second a boat, and the care of the poet is to keep his *horse* or his *boat* from
> *singing*.
>
> Samuel Johnson, *Life of Addison*[1]

There is a sense in which the examples cited so far do not offer any
linguistic difficulties; and one in which metaphors seem to do so.
The difference is often supposed to lie in a distinction between the
literal and the figurative uses of language. Thus if we compare

> John put on his friendliest and most sincere expression and
> walked toward the man

with

> the sweet small clumsy feet of April came
> into the ragged meadow of my soul[2]

we feel that the former has a direct and explicable relationship to its
situation or possible state of affairs, whereas the latter has not. And
yet both make assertions.[3] The grounds of this contrast are very
difficult to specify in the present state of our knowledge,[4] even
though mature speakers do seem to be able to say with certainty
which are metaphorical uses of language.[5] We may then be able to
make the initial hypothesis that we internalize 'normal' uses of
language and can recognize figurative language as a 'deviant' use
which is in some way foregrounded against these literal norms.[6]

I follow Max Black in using the terminology of 'focus' for the
deviating component, and 'frame' for the literal language which
surrounds it.[7] Thus for the examples

> The chairman ploughed through the discussion

and

> The ship ploughs the sea

'ploughed' and 'ploughs' are the foci, and yet there could be literal
ways of filling in the frame (with 'slept', 'took notes', 'sails', and so
on). This mode of analysis has of course no great rigour. It can only
be used to suggest part of the psychological process by which we
may recognize that we have a metaphor to deal with.

A further clue to our recognition of metaphors seems once more to be cognitive : in relationship to the context of situation provided by the text (which in some cases, such as proverbs, may be the world as a whole), we see that the statement involved cannot literally be true, or cannot be true if its terms are taken in some primary sense without interpretation. Thus once we stop to consider how strange it is, we find that metaphor may seem to be perversely asserting something which is plainly known not to be the case, as in 'The Lord is my Shepherd, I shall not want', or 'Men are verbs not nouns' or 'All the world's a stage'. We may say that the months of the year do not literally have feet, and that souls, whatever they may or may not be, certainly aren't meadows, that chairmen aren't agriculturalists, and so on. By 'literally' here, we mean 'as a matter of fact'. We may thus distinguish between judgements expressing likeness as literal or metaphorical in relation to their truth-claims.[8]
Thus

Encyclopaedias are like dictionaries
is thought literally true, and

Encyclopaedias are like gold mines
is not literally true, but only so 'in a way'. Our aim in interpreting these non-literal uses of language seems to be to save them from falsity. If we leave them alone we leave them to say something false. (The same consideration may apply to irony.) We have to consult the ordinary meaning of the words to add to the sentence what it doesn't say but implies, and our problem is to put a sensible limit to those implications.

Metaphor is thus recognized in context, and its construal is part of the pragmatics of discourse. Once we know what it is for something to be a metaphorical statement, i.e. the contexts in which people make such statements intending them to be meaningful, relevant to other statements, and so on, then we can judge that a metaphorical reading is preferable to a literal one. Of course the way in which we come at this judgement, that by saying 'S is P' a speaker or writer really means 'S is R' is very complicated.[9]

How then do we arrive at a metaphorical interpretation? Suppose we have the sentence

The coroner was confronted by a smokescreen of witnesses.
We might locate 'smokescreen' as the (non-literal) focus of our attention : and claim that the witnesses were *like* a smokescreen in that 'they made it very difficult to find out what actually happened'. We know that witnesses are supposed to help make things clear, and these perhaps deliberately did not. I argue that if my explanation of this metaphor is so far acceptable (and shows that I have understood it) it is so on two main grounds : (1) I have paraphrased

it in some way. Obviously enough, it is no reply to the question 'What do you understand by X?' in this context, simply to reiterate 'X'. The second ground is more controversial. I suggest that (2) the paraphrase should be in a language closer than the original to that in which we might assess truth-claims. In terms of our argument earlier, it should draw our attention to specific facts or generally acceptable propositions within the schemas for the text. We see that the paraphrase expresses part of the meaning we take to have been intended, because the truth-conditions are the same. The para-phrase may thus specify the relationship of the original assertion to an implied situation. It is context-dependent. This formulation is in fact a very guarded one, for reasons that will emerge more fully later. I suggest not that the figurative passage will paraphrase into true statements, but into statements for which we hypothetically might be able to assess truth or falsity. This qualification is necessary for two basic reasons. Firstly, we might never actually be able to arrive at a completely satisfactory truth-telling language; and secondly, partly in consequence of this, our assessment of truth-claims inside and outside literature (in co-text and in context) may never be absolutely certain, but relative to the norms in force, within particular groups, for the assessment of such claims. I would nevertheless be surprised if my paraphrase of the 'smokescreen' focus was not thought acceptable on both grounds.

The context-dependent nature of my interpretation is shown by the fact that I selected some aspects of my knowledge of smoke-screens (that they may be deliberately caused, that they obscure vision) and that finding out what happened (the job of a coroner) is virtually, i.e. non-metaphorically, like seeing what happened. But at the same time I suppressed other facts (that smokescreens billow about, that they may be brown or grey, and so on), which are not relevant implications for my interpretation. In Black's terms, I have exploited the 'system of associated commonplaces' (cf. 'frame') for the term involved (and appealed also to the relevant schemata for it).[10]

This overriding or cancellation of some of the semantic markers or conceptual features of words seems to be at least typical of metaphor (as, for example, personification overrides the animate/inanimate distinction). It might be thought that the study of metaphor could be made at least more rigorous by ranking these features. Thus Cohen hypothesized that in metaphorical cases, 'empirical' rather than 'inferential' features were cancelled.[11] For a sentence like

This legislative programme is a rocket to the moon

we would cancel such obvious empirical features of the frame for 'rocket' as 'material', and 'air-cleaving' and 'cylindrical', but keep such inferred features as 'fast-moving' and 'far-arriving'. But Cohen found this unsatisfactory, preferring to argue that semantic features should be arranged in an 'order of decreasing semantic importance', and that metaphor could be found to cancel the most important, general, and obvious ones, and retain the 'more distinctive and specific' ones which were less probable and carried more information.[12]

However there are a number of objections to this sort of approach which I think make it not worth pursuing. For an appeal to semantic features and so on is empirically no more certain than more informal approaches. It is all very well to talk of 'sortal incorrectness' in 'logical space' or of 'psycho-lexical space',[13] but we know very little about the actual psychological organization of our semantic memories, or of the hierarchical way in which we organize language associatively 'in our heads'. It is difficult to be clear about hierarchies within frames.

This is because it soon becomes clear that when such semantic features are actually specified, they mix very general 'philosophical' categories which seem logically plausible and generally necessary (like the animate/inanimate distinction) with empirical knowledge and beliefs which are not strictly part of our linguistic competence at all.[14] The ranking of semantic features attempted by many linguists is thus not nearly as rigorous or enlightening as it looks. Their ordering is uncertain; their degree of generality in relation to one another is uncertain; and they ultimately, usually in the 'lower' reaches, express some general knowledge of the objects or states of affairs referred to by the term to be analysed. (The crucial function of this general knowledge will emerge in what follows.)

There is a further objection to the notion that metaphor can be successfully analysed by exclusive reference to the overriding or violation of linguistically defined selection restrictions.[15] This is simply that there seem to be exceptions: cases in which the sentence does not involve any such violation in itself but brings them about in relation to context. Thus Reddy points out that

The rock is becoming brittle with age

is literal in a geological context and metaphorical if its context of reference is to a professor emeritus.[16] Conversely, the 'deviant' sentence is not necessarily metaphorical, and so

The tree asked Mervyn to direct it to London

could be literal in a fantasy-world like that of *Lord of the Rings* in which trees are animate and articulate.[17] Selectional violations of this kind may simply in some contexts refer to deviant worlds. And such pragmatic contexts could not of course be specified in advance by a linguistic theory. A further objection to overriding as a key to the nature of metaphor is far simpler. As we may expect from our analysis of implication in relatively straightforward prose, focus interpretations of metaphor do not differ essentially from those we find for literal expressions. In both cases we select those features which are compatible with the context and suppress those which are not. It is thus unlikely that models of language alone will take us as far as we need to go in the interpretation of metaphor; and this conclusion has consequences for any formalist or linguistic theory of interpretation. But what further elements are likely to be needed? We may be able to specify them if we go back to some more examples. And granted that our empirical knowledge is going to be involved, we ought to return to our criterion of relevance to a situation.

We can see how such a criterion of appropriacy will help us to select relevant associations for the focused terms of metaphor if we look at ambiguous expressions such as the following

I had a cloudy thought.

The poor are the negroes of Europe. (Chamfort)

We can paraphrase the first sentence in two ways, as meaning either 'the sort of thought that is vague and obscure, as a cloud is ill-defined and opaque' or as 'the sort of thought which precedes depression as the (rain-cloud) precedes bad weather' (with a further metaphorical equivalence implied between depression and bad weather). Our criterion for appropriacy in interpretation must include that of adequacy to, and coherence with, the situation of the text (the co-text). And so on for examples of increasing complexity.

The second example is slightly more complicated since it also involves an appeal to our awareness of types of speech act. 'Negroes' is the focus and so we have to think of (factual) aspects of the Negro condition, presumably in the America of Chamfort's time, that might apply where appropriate to the condition of the poor in Europe. We thus appeal to a potentially large body of knowledge. But the selective aspects of the truth condition can be seen to be relevant here if we note that they will differ radically if we construe the sentence, taken as a speech act, as either dismissive ('The poor are merely . . .') or as deprecatory ('The poor suffer from the same deplorable injustices as . . .'). We rely again on some pretty commonplace knowledge to work out the grounds of comparison; though of course the rhetorical force of the metaphor lies in our discovery of those features of the treatment of Negroes that we had not, until Chamfort implied them, thought to apply to the poor (as perhaps a 'race apart', or as somehow genetically inferior, and so on).

The case of the ambiguous metaphor (and by extension of the

ambiguous text) helps to clarify why I said that the paraphrase interpretation should be one whose language is closer than that of the metaphor to that in which we make truth-claims. For it is *only* by using this more perspicuous language that we can judge whether two or more competing interpretations of a metaphor are more or less appropriate to the external situation to which it refers us (its context) or to which it helps to project within a fiction (its co-text). Metaphorical interpretation is thus a particular case of pragmatic implication.

Thus metaphors do not state truths (they are 'literally' false), but they do imply them for the interpreter. And we fit them to the world (real or imagined) by selecting those features they imply which are appropriate to a situation. Put another way, our understanding of figurative language essentially involves 'reality-testing', and a form of testing which will provide some degree of certainty. (This will give rise to a general thesis concerning the relationship of text to world in Chapter 4.) The question then arises whether we can paraphrase a metaphor with any certainty or according to any rules or conventions, and whether there is any basic underlying conceptual structure for them, to which we may appeal.

One line of analysis attempts to show that there may be linguistic rules by which we may transfer meaning from one word to another. Thus Geoffrey Leech argues that 'language contains rules of transference, or particular mechanisms for deriving one meaning of a word from another.'[18] He separates out of the metaphor what he calls, following Richards, the tenor (and I shall continue to call the literal frame) and the vehicle (which I shall continue to call the focus). He thus shows that Chaucer's

> But ye loveres that bathen in gladnesse

can be divided into a literal frame or tenor

> But ye loveres that —— gladnesse

and a figurative focus or vehicle

> —— bathen in ——

For both of these, literal terms can be substituted thus

> But ye loveres that (feel) gladnesse
> But ye loveres that bathen in (water)

Literal terms can similarly be substituted for

>   The sky rejoices in the morning's birth

so that the literal frame may read

>   The sky (looks bright at) the morning's (beginning)

and the figurative focus

>   (Animate noun, human) rejoices in (animate's) birth[19]

Leech's 'rule' for analysis is to avoid inserting further figurative expressions in the paraphrases, and having done so, to look for a *ground of likeness* by asking what similarity can be discerned between the top and bottom lines of the analysis. Thus the brightness of the sky is like rejoicing (on the grounds that the correlation between brightness and cheerfulness is a commonplace). Dawn is like a birth (in that both are beginnings), and so on. Leech goes on to claim that 'This method shows clearly that tenor and vehicle, i.e. the things compared in the metaphor are not usually identified with the literal or figurative sense of particular words: often one whole clause is placed in opposition to another.'[20] This is also important for showing that a metaphorical sentence may have more than one focus, so that both tenor and vehicle may need metaphorical interpretation. Thus both 'bathen' and 'gladnesse' could be taken as the focus of the Chaucer example, as is in fact tacitly shown by Leech in giving literal substitutes for both terms.

The way in which both frame and focus may interact so that both require interpretation is shown in a more complex example cited by Reinhart, from Eliot's 'Prufrock'[21]

>   The yellow fog that rubs its back upon the window panes

The primary focus here seems to be 'rubs its back upon' for which we can substitute the more literal 'touches like a cat', and so on. But it is the fog, which occurs literally in the original sentence, that is also like a cat, in that it is, for example, indeterminate in shape, fuzzy in texture, and so on. Thus the fog touches the window like a cat in X respects, and is also like a cat in Y respects. Reinhart points out that our interpretation of the fog–cat equivalence adds something to the text—an image:

Since in this metaphor both concepts are concrete, the image is rich in visual options—we can imagine a yellow cat and a yellow fog, both are in motion.

There can be a similarity between the fuzziness of the cat's fur and the texture of the fog. The fog may be associated with a certain warmth, or even friendliness : there is something sensuous about the fog, which ties in with the atmosphere of the poem.[22]

The basic rule that seems to emerge from this type of analysis is this: the figurative term of the text being interpreted is like the literal ones of the paraphrase implied by it *in certain specific respects*. Thus a cloud is like a thought in that both can be vague and obscure, and, one supposes, feeling gladness is like bathing in that both are, say, pleasurably engulfing and warmly enclosing experiences, particularly if one is making love (though this paraphrase indicates the dominance of metaphor over our description of mental experiences). I think that this 'likeness in respects' rule is acceptable as a mode of paraphrase for metaphors, even though, as we shall see, not all metaphors assert likeness, and it is rather too vague to be much of a rule. For the force of the paraphrase lies not simply in the bringing-out of an implied assertion of likeness but in its discrimination of the grounds which license it. This is in fact the key to all transactions by the interpreter between the text and the world.

The bringing to light of such comparisons is not of course in any sense an emotional, imagistic, or rhetorical equivalent of metaphor. They only show part of the way in which we might understand it. For, as I shall argue throughout, interpretation changes the meaning of texts by putting them in other words, and is only justifiable for specified pragmatic purposes, in this case, that of showing how metaphors may imply truthful propositions (likenesses grounded by respects) about their situations.

What then is the status of these appeals to similarity or likeness in interpreting metaphor? We need to make a little clearer what we are doing when we appeal to likeness and its grounds. As we have already suggested, it is the actual *selection* of a ground that makes the metaphor intelligible. For, as Searle points out, 'Similarity is a common predicate: any two things are similar in some respects or other. Saying that the metaphor 'S is P' implies the literal 'S is like P' does not solve our problem, it only pushes it back a step.'[23] If Juliet is like the sun she is neither gaseous nor 90 million miles away, but something else. But is there a reliable way of arriving at this something else? This leads to another objection recorded by Searle, that although the grounds we appeal to may seem interpretatively rational, our statement of them involves a psychological process of 'calling to mind' which is very difficult to specify (compare the difficulty of making a frame or semantic field 'psychologically real'). For if when we say 'S is P' and somehow convey 'S is R', 'the hard problem is to explain what exactly are the principles according to which an utterance of an expression can metaphorically call to mind a different set of truth conditions from the one determined by its literal meaning, and to state those principles precisely and without using metaphorical expressions like "call to mind".'[24]

We may in fact be asking a rather vague question, like 'How does one thing remind us of another?' or 'How does a concept activate its frame?' However if we look at a fair number of metaphors, as Searle does, we find that there do seem to be some fairly standard answers to this question. Metaphors may not have standard linguistic patterns underlying them, but they do seem to have at least some standard logical or inferential patterns. For example 'Sam is a giant' can be taken to mean 'Sam is big' because giants are *by definition* big, or 'Richard is a gorilla' may mean 'Richard is mean nasty and prone to violence' because gorillas are *often said or believed to be* like this (even though in fact they are not).[25]

Although analyses of this kind may clarify the logical structure of the grounds to which we appeal in the interpretation of metaphor, it should be noted that once again they consistently appeal to our knowledge—to the known properties of things or to what is believed for cultural or other reasons. In our last example 'gorilla mythology' provided the relevant associations. Interpretation is thus culturally relative. As Paul Henle points out, 'A popular song of some years ago praised a young lady by saying that "You're the cream in my coffee". Entirely the wrong impression would be obtained in a community which drank its coffee black.'[26] The grounds of likeness in metaphors thus involve all sorts of conventions of reference to the real world; and these could never be specified in advance by a linguistic or any other theory, or by the analysis even of typical inference patterns.[27] Metaphor consists in the implication by likeness of a certain description of the world, which is rationalized or justified by its grounds—and the acceptability of these implications depends ultimately upon the nature of the world, or if one prefers, upon the nature of our beliefs about it. It is (as we shall see later, in more detail) the function of the interpreter to mediate between the text and these beliefs, and in some cases to provide the relevant knowledge.

Thus, as Black points out, it will depend on how much we know, whether we interpret

Marriage is a zero sum game

as implying that since a game is a contest between opponents in which one can win only at the expense of the other, then marriage is also a contest in which rewards are gained at the expense of one's partner; or whether we interpret it in a more sophisticated way through game theory, as implying that 'there is no rational procedure for winning in a single play' and so on.[28] It is the attempt to bring comparably esoteric knowledge of this kind within a reader's compass that accounts for much critical interpretation. We can see how this is for a relatively simple case if we look at an example from Yeats:

> Plato thought nature but a spume that plays
> Upon a ghostly paradigm of things.

This comes from 'Among School Children'. We are expected to know enough about Plato's theory of Forms to see the appropriacy of Yeats's metaphorical restatement, where 'spume' and 'plays' have a dismissive force. 'Ghostly paradigm' will cause some trouble with its grammatical rather than philosophical associations (though even these seem in a way appropriate) unless we know that Yeats has incorporated into his own idiolect Thomas Taylor's use of 'paradigm' to mean 'archetype or essence', that is Platonic Form.[29] We can then reconstruct the philosophic model or schema for the sentence from Yeats's terms. A crude paraphrase might run as follows :

Plato thought nature (i.e. the material visible world, by knowledge of Plato's system) was no more than an inessential by-product (like the frothy foam on the edge of the sea), which plays upon (i.e. plays no essential function with respect to, and is perpetually changing) the really existent though ghostly paradigm (which according to Plato is not immediately visible, is above and beyond nature, and remains accessible only to philosophical contemplation) that is the essential framework (indeed the grammatical paradigm) of the Forms, which transcend the material appearances of things (as the ghost represents the essential outline of a person without his material body).

Of course the force of the metaphor lies not so much in its closeness to the Platonic doctrines which are teased out of it by this clumsy paraphrase, as in its deviance from them. For instead of implying the static Platonic view of the world as composed of commonplace objects (like beds) whose form or archetype is only accessible to philosophic contemplation, Yeats goes beyond this to present a view of the world as a whole as perpetually changing and fickle like the spray of the sea, mere 'froth upon the daydream', to borrow Vian's phrase. The original version of these lines was much weaker and more orthodox:

> Plato imagined all existence plays
> Among the ghostly images of things.[30]

The relevance of this particular statement to its imagined situation of utterance, as the meditation of a 'sixty-year-old smiling public man' in a school classroom on the pretensions of the intellect, is a matter for interpretation of the stanza in the co-text of the poem as a whole. It is nevertheless by virtue of our having a 'cultural convention' concerning the nature of Plato's theories (in the 'encyclopaedia') and of later modifications of them, that we have a check on our paraphrase interpretation of these lines. The cultural norms implicit here and right through the stanza include that which accepts Plato, Aristotle, and Pythagoras as having laid the foundations for all later speculative philosophical thinking.

Our interpretation of metaphor in problematic or literary contexts is thus not likely to depend on any appeal to the internal organization of language, but to be contingent upon the nature of our beliefs concerning the world and its history. The search for the acceptable implications of a metaphor will involve a large range of conventions of reference, description, and likeness as regards the way in which the objects, persons, and events and qualities of the metaphor figure in our experience (including that of literature). But a further and sceptical question now arises : what is the status of these conventions to which I have so confidently appealed? What in particular is the status of the distinction between 'literal' and 'metaphorical' on which we rely, when we think of the interpretative paraphrase as mediating the relationship of the (figurative) text to the (literally describable) world?

2.2 Metaphor in the Language

The truth is that there are no ultimate principles, upon which the whole of knowledge can be built once and forever as upon a rock. But there are an infinity of analogues, which help us along, and give a feeling of power over the chaos when we perceive them. The field is infinite and herein lies the chance for originality. Here there are some new things under the sun.

T. E. Hulme, 'Cinders'[1]

I have argued so far that the interpretation of particular metaphors looks for grounds of explication at a level that both interpreter and reader may accept. There is a sense in which any refusal to accept the interpretation of the examples given so far could be taken to reflect a basic ignorance of the way things are in the world or in our culture—clouds are opaque, 'ghostly paradigms' are like Platonic forms, and so on. An agreed notion of what is the case seems to be operative here, and although we have accepted that there can be no final restriction of what these states of affairs might be, we have implied that there can be conventions of reference which guarantee both the acceptability of an interpretation, and an intelligible and possibly truth-conveying relationship between metaphor and the world. But in doing so we accord to the supposedly more literal language of interpretation a privileged form of access to reality. In the *simple* cases, this seems all right—to reflect a state of affairs which 'no rational person would seek to deny'. But there are more difficult cases, which may also be fundamental ones, for which it may be doubted that we have arrived, or indeed ever could arrive, at this type of literal, universally acceptable interpretation. Even apparently literal statements about the world or the situation within or beyond the text may in fact depend upon metaphorical types of model-building : ways of seeing the world which, when examined closely, no longer look all that literal. For, in analysing our language down to an apparently literal level we may arrive at a new series of metaphors which themselves stand in need of interpretation, and which may stand in the way of any finally satisfactory, literal, well-founded relationship of language to the world.

We admitted at the outset that the distinction between literal and metaphorical usage was a very hard one to draw; but suggested that the 'literal' expression—in the language at large, or in the paraphrases we use to clarify metaphor, were in some way more 'immediately verifiable'. Although the metaphor sets us off on a detour, we travel through it to a relatively stable relationship to a situation. Thus kings and reason may both (literally) exert some kind of control, hence 'sovran reason'; smokescreens are literally opaque; Plato did believe that particulars and Forms were related in a certain way. This detour towards the literal seems to offer a degree of certainty in interpretation, since likeness and ground of likeness stated in 'literal' language seemed to offer us access to a world of stable facts. The basic force of this appeal lies, as we shall see, in *agreement*—upon arriving at a point at which interpretation may reasonably stop, as there seem to be no further ambiguities or complications to explicate in the context, and the interpreter and reader can accept a relationship between language and the external world. (They share the relevant beliefs.)

However, Jacques Derrida argues that there is no such stopping-place; since the notion of literality upon which I have founded it is a false one. His argument is addressed mainly to the hidden metaphorical language of philosophy,[2] but it has equally severe consequences for literary interpretation. One would expect the language of philosophy to be maximally explicit (to be as literal as possible) and not to offer the problems of interpretation we find in the figurative language of the literary text. Derrida attempts to destroy this expectation, by pointing out that philosophy (and hence all uses of language, including our paraphrase explications of metaphor) is full of the 'white mythology' of hidden metaphor : 'the metaphor is no longer noticed, and is taken for the proper meaning.'[3] 'Proper meaning' is for Derrida something like the ideal given up by Wittgenstein after the *Tractatus*, of a purely referential and wholly reliable use of language.

Derrida thus revives in an apparently new guise one of the most traditional views of language—that in Shelleyan terms it is 'vitally metaphorical' from its primitive origins, and remains so.[4] We fail to realize this because the 'wear' upon each of our favoured, coin-like metaphors has effaced from them 'the fabulous scene which brought it into being'.[5] Our approach to language must therefore be a critical one, in the tradition of Renan, Nietzsche, Freud, Bergson, and Lenin, 'who were conscious of metaphorical activity in theoretical or philosophical discourse'.[6] Nietzsche in particular is quoted with approval—'What then is truth? a mobile army of metaphors, metonymies, anthropomorphisms . . . illusions which have forgotten that they are illusions'.[7] The reference to illusion reveals that the approach is a sceptical one—our language will perpetually lead us astray unless we scrutinize it for these hidden metaphorical models. As Paul Ricœur points out in his excellent discussion of Derrida: 'La déconstruction Heideggérienne doit maintenant s'adjoindre la généalogie nietzschéenne, la psychanalyse freudienne, la critique marxiste de l'idéologie, c'est à dire les armes de l'herméneutique du soupçon. Ainsi armée, la critique est en mesure de démasquer la conjonction *impensée* de la métaphysique *dissimulée* et de la métaphore usée.'[8]

Derrida's aim thus seems to be to revive the dead metaphors of philosophy : so that we may 'read in a concept the hidden history of metaphor.'[9] To this end he refers unsurprisingly to Pierre Louis's *Les Métaphores de Platon*, for as is well known, classical philosophy was eclectic in its sources and drew from them biological, organic, and mechanical metaphors. The result is that the basic ideas of philosophy (*theoria, eidos, logos,* and so on) may themselves be susceptible of philosophical reinterpretation : there is no reliable foundation or bedrock (to compound the metaphor) for our discourse. Indeed, 'concept is a metaphor, foundation is a metaphor; theory is a metaphor; and there is no metametaphor for them.'[10] As Ricœur points out, the paradox is that we cannot talk about metaphor except by using a conceptual network which is itself engendered out of metaphor.[11] We have already in this section used concepts like those of *grounds* of likeness, the *reflection* of ignorance, our *access* to reality, our seeing the world under a certain *aspect*, our going through a metaphorical *detour*. How far do Derrida's arguments count against such usages? For language will never rise to that impossible ideal of literality and certainty which Derrida despairs of, and objectivist philosophy in general wishes to impose upon it : 'To be univocal is the essence, or rather the *telos*, of language. This Aristotelian ideal has never been rejected by any philosophy as such. It is philosophy.'[12]

Derrida is undoubtedly correct in seeing metaphor as buried within philosophy (and hence within theoretical and critical discourse) : what one may doubt is whether there is much point in resurrecting it in the way he suggests. Is it really the case, for example, that in the normal use of the word 'concept' by philosophers and educational psychologists or critics there really is still the 'pattern of the gesture of power . . . the grasping or taking hold of the thing as an object'?[13]

What I wish to suggest at this stage is that although we may be reminded of the historically based metaphorical etymologies of the words we use, their function in the ordinary day-to-day negotiation we make between language and the world may not be much affected by these facts, unless they are critically brought to our consciousness, for a clearly defined critical *purpose*. For words which had an original basis in metaphor become 'lexicalized' as Ricœur argues with reference to Le Guern.[14] Although the French 'tête' may come from the Latin 'testa' or 'little pot', in actual usage 'tête' just is the proper word ('le mot propre') for 'head' in French. We may come to define the 'literal' sense of such a word as at least its usual or agreed sense in context with other words: 'Il n'est donc pas besoin d'une métaphysique du propre pour justifier la différence du littéral et du figuré; c'est l'emploi dans le discours, et non je ne sais quel prestige du primitif ou de l'originel, qui spécifie la différence du littéral et du métaphorique'.[15]

Thus one line of defence against Derrida may seem to be to say that the historical analysis of language may be very interesting, but the language seems to be functioning very well for practical purposes without our paying any attention to such facts. For us, 'concept' means 'an idea in the head', or whatever the Oxford English Dictionary says it means, or whatever a philosopher may persuade us it means, and we need not concern ourselves too much with its origin as 'the taking hold of a thing'. No more do we take hold of things when we comprehend : indeed comprehending may not have so much to do with taking hold as with another metaphor, that of 'knowing how to go on' which is the way in which Wittgenstein, for example, partly defines our notion of understanding.[16]

This seems all right as far as it goes; but it disregards the deeper *ideological* aims of this type of analysis, aims to which we will have to pay a good deal of attention in what follows. For Derridan analysis may reveal a use of concepts with hidden metaphorical levels which are *systematic* in some way that reveals the nature of those general beliefs about the world to which we appeal in interpreting metaphor, and of which we are hardly conscious, because they are so deeply encoded in the language we use to deal with the text. (To put the matter very crudely, suppose that the use of 'concept' as a hidden way of saying 'taking hold' was related to a whole system of ways in which we talk about knowledge as possession, so that our usual ways of thinking were based upon a series of metaphors which suggested that 'knowledge is proprietary power'.)

There is thus a dialectic within our interpretation of language, and our interpretation of interpretation : one of which appeals to normal procedures and to the meanings of language in use, and takes them to be in a satisfactory relationship to the text and the world (which runs the risk of ideological complacency) and the other which takes a more critical approach to the underlying metaphorical structures of language (and thus runs the risk of an infinite regress as the explanation of metaphor is found to contain more metaphors, which in turn have to be explained).

This critical analysis of metaphorical structures within ordinary language has recently been undertaken by Lakoff and Johnson.[17] It is worth giving some account of it here, as critics have traditionally found very similar structures underlying the literary text. They argue that our conceptual system as a whole is structured by metaphors, which provide systematic and coherent models for whole areas of discourse. These models emerge very clearly for example when we see that the way in which we talk about winning or losing arguments owes a great deal to the metaphorical model of 'war', or that theories and arguments are spoken of in terms of buildings,[18] or that we talk about time which may be 'expended' or 'wasted' as if it were money.[19] Thus *in our culture* but not necessarily in others, we tend to treat time as a valuable commodity—and one can imagine reasons for this. Thus Lakoff and Johnson pursue Derrida-like considerations into much more informal types of discourse, in which love may be seen as a kind of journey, and so on.[20] These metaphorical models are, they argue, quite wide-rangingly systematic.

The pervasiveness of such metaphorical models shows that, in ordinary language as much as in literature, we perpetually structure one type of experience in terms of another. Likeness is fundamental to our most abstract ways of thinking. We say 'tell me the story of your life', and accept the underlying model—life is structured like a story : it should have, or we should find in it, a coherent narrative. We can ask whether this type of coherence (with stages, goals, plans, selected causal relations) really matches the course of a life. This, and the peculiar consequence of giving an affirmative answer, preoccupies Sartre in *La Nausée*. Or we may understand love, for example, not simply in terms of its inherent properties, such as fondness, affection, and sexual desire, but also in terms of its organizing metaphors, which have 'interactional properties'.[21] Thus Lakoff and Johnson argue that our concepts are not just the foci of sets of (definitional) properties, but 'structured gestalts' which exploit likenesses.[22]

Anyone who has read some love poetry can see that our discourse concerning love can be structured in even more specialized ways. And we can see systematic metaphorical implications in more ordinary but more powerful political discourse : as when a leader declares 'war' on inflation (with all the discomforts and 'necessary sacrifice' that that may entail).

Arguments of this kind use their very wide range of evidence concerning metaphorical structures in language to a philosophical end which is very close to Derrida's implied attack on 'objectivity' and the 'metaphysics of presence' (of which more later). They wish to show that our reliance on a myth of objective literal truth is

unfounded, and that as Derrida himself suggests, with respect to the
language of philosophy, we always see the world relative to a
conceptual scheme defined largely by metaphor.[23] The implication
of this is, that once we recognize their metaphorical status, the area
in which we are 'objective' and not seduced or guided by
metaphorical models is very limited. Thus our understanding is
always relative to the underlying models and to our purposes in
using them in particular situations. ('We understand a statement as
being true in a given situation when our understanding of the
statement fits our understanding of the situation closely enough for
our purposes.'[24]) Our understanding is always relative to these
systems or frameworks, which are shot through with metaphor, even
in the case of science, where it uses models. This is the best we can
do. We will thus depend not alone on the correspondence of our
statements to situations, but also upon a potentially shifting series of
models for conceptual coherence, whose evolution and use will
ultimately depend on their success in dealing with the environment.[25] Different types of cultural assumptions will mediate between
our language and reality. They will so mediate because we are not
just dealing with objects—sticks and stones—but also with social,
political, religious, and literary institutions with their own specialized models, and these are just as 'real' as physical objects.[26] It is
thus impossible to give an objectivist theory of truth, and in
particular any objectivist attempt to make metaphors stay dead will
ultimately fail, for any attempt to assign a metaphorical and a literal
sense to words will disregard metaphorical entailments.[27] Our
understanding of the world thus takes place within a framework of
competing, and not necessarily even consistent, metaphorical
systems, many of which are of course strongly reinforced by the
institutions of religion, myth, and literature.[28] The distinction
between a literal and a metaphorical use of words is thus a
pragmatic one, that we make in various circumstances for various
ends. It can not be finally adjudicated by theoretical argument (for
there is no reason *ex hypothesi* to believe in the first place that a
consistent language could be found in which to conduct it). This is a
situation in which we are free to choose between language uses, and
need not be coerced by theoretical considerations; and it will be
found to recur in the practice of interpretation. Thus Derrida's
attempt to revive dead metaphors, or that of deconstruction to show
that metaphors may misleadingly underly the structure of the
literary text (cf. Chapter 4), have a particular force as critiques of
our basic assumptions about the language we use. But they cannot
show that such assumptions were either wholly ill-founded, or
ineffective for the purposes they served.

Thus our critical awareness of, say, the building metaphor for arguments, need not prevent us from making intelligible assessments of their 'structure' and 'well-founded' use. We would in any case, if we are going to continue to have the practice of antagonistic argument (like this one) need to continue to use such words to mark our assessments of such arguments. And if Derrida and Lakoff and Johnson are right, even if we tried to 'purify' our language, we would inevitably find ourselves using another set of metaphors (which deconstructive criticism could show to be equally misleading in some respects). If we want to keep the institution of argument or critical theory going at all, we will have to accept that some such norms derived from metaphorical structure will be in force. If we manage to know (pragmatically) where we are with them we may be all right—though we will also have to accept that such norms change through time, partly or largely as a response to criticism of the Derridan kind.

These considerations, so far as they affect our notion of objectivity or truth in interpretation, will have to be pursued further at a later stage. What is important for our purposes here is to recognize that interpretation of metaphorical language in texts will both reveal and be subject to models of explanation and understanding which are themselves metaphorically modelled. It has been one of the most exciting and revolutionary aspects of the new interpretation, as it has been informed by structuralism, post-structuralism, and semiotics, that it has begun to look at these underlying systems within language. This is not simply to reveal them for what they are (as all-pervasive) but also to reflect upon their underlying purposes with respect to beliefs and ideology, of which we may be largely unconscious. In what follows I wish to develop what we have learnt here concerning literal and metaphorical language to the more extended level of the literary text as a whole.

3.1 Linguistics and Interpretation

In our discussion of metaphor in relation to interpretation, we saw that it had a double aspect : (1) it was interpretable into a 'literal' language exploiting 'grounds of likeness' which might reveal certain systematic (associative) features within language, and thus be part of larger-scale metaphorical models, thereby (2) opening up all sorts of possible conventions of reference from the literary text to the external world (its context of situation). We also saw the beginnings of arguments against these propositions, which asserted that there were no such reliable stopping-places for interpretation, since all language is ultimately metaphorical.

These opposed views of the nature of interpretation lead further on in two directions, which I shall explore in this and the next chapter. The first leads us to examine what we shall call the 'coherence-conferring' version of structuralism, which relates the larger features of the text to systems within language which are the conditions for literary meanings and thus make possible, so it is asserted, a descriptive science of literature, or 'poétique'. The second direction, that taken by 'post-structuralist' critics, seems entirely opposed to this. It criticizes the very basis of our trust in the literary sign, and thus leads us to believe that literary texts, far from being models or examples of coherent linguistic structures, whose conventions can be stated with some finality, are self-contradictory, fissured, and full of gaps, and do not allow for any static stopping-point in interpretation.

We thus come to look at features of the literary work which are on a larger scale than that of metaphor or of the single sentence which usually encloses it, but which are subject to the same basic interpretative procedures.

An unrigorous notion of the unifying structure of poetry has long been available to literary criticism, as will be seen if we consider my fairly simple analysis of a poem by E. E. Cummings:[1]

> if everything happens that can't be done
> (and anything's righter
> than books
> could plan)
> the stupidest teacher will almost guess
> (with a run
> skip

around we go yes)
there's nothing as something as one

one hasn't a why or because or although
(and buds know better
than books
don't grow)
one's anything old being everything new
(with a what
which
around we come who)
one's everyanything so

so world is a leaf so tree is a bough
(and birds sing sweeter
than books
tell how)
so here is away and so your is a my
(with a down
up
around again fly)
forever was never till now

now i love you and you love me
(and books are shuter
than books
can be)
and deep in the high that does nothing but fall
(with a shout
each
around we go all)
there's somebody calling who's we

we're anything brighter than even the sun
(we're everything greater
than books
might mean)
we're everyanything more than believe
(with a spin
leap
alive we're alive)
we're wonderful one times one

Here the long lines carry the argument, as we can see if we insert (in
brackets) the implied logical relationships between stanzas : 'if
everything happens ... (and) one hasn't a why ... so (that the)
world is a leaf ... (and) now I love you ... (then) we're anything
brighter than even the sun ... we're wonderful one times one'. We

begin with 'everything' happening, and end with the single 'one times one' of the lovers. Enclosed within these lines are two further thematically unified sequences : a repeated dispraise of books—everything is righter than them, birds know better than them so shut them, because (the lovers are) greater than them, and a counter-posed family of physical actions—running, skipping, flying, shouting, springing, and leaping, to show climactically that 'alive we're alive', where the very word 'alive' runs round itself.

Thus there are in fact three parallel arguments within a stanza which is a beautiful rhythmic and syllabic repetition of itself. The rhyme is varyingly inset (*a b c a d e f d a*) so that the first, fourth, and ninth lines rhyme or half rhyme, and so do the fifth and eighth lines, the second line always containing a comparative, and the third always ending 'books'.

Of course analysis reveals this structure, and could do similar things for pretty well any poem. One of the questions I wish to ask concerning it is simple, but hard to answer. What is the relationship between this kind of formal description and the actual process of our understanding and interpretation of the text?

We may wish to say, for example, that such literary structures function subliminally in our reading, as when for example we 'recognize' that the second series of brackets are all like one another in that they describe free physical actions (i.e. a process like that in our recognition of metaphor is involved).[2] For this one would need a theory of language which asserted both (1) that there were semantic fields concerning, say, books and physical actions, and (2) that these were somehow 'psychologically real' and thus functional within the reading of the text.[3] Some such view would have to underpin, for example, the Lakoff and Johnson thesis that our conceptions of various aspects of reality like love and arguing were in fact already structured by interacting metaphors. This interaction would be supposed to be in our heads as well as in the language, so that we were to some degree 'programmed' by our own language.

Nearly all our problems concerning the status of interpretations which depend upon the postulation or demonstration of such underlying linguistic structures in a text, from Jakobson to Riffaterre and beyond, will depend upon our attitude to these two assertions. What we have said so far concerning the function of frameworks and schemas, our ability to scan through the 'system of associated commonplaces' in metaphor, and concerning the systematic meta-phorical structures in language, tends towards a positive answer to the question concerning psychological reality; even if as we noted, the attempt to put such frameworks into a logical hierarchic order may be doomed to failure.

For the concept of the semantic field does seem to have a particularly important function to play in our analysis of the linguistic structure of the text. For the text may be seen to exploit a 'linguistic system' even if this does not correspond in any very easily specifiable way to the organization of semantic memory, or to the master-metaphors within language.

This approach to the text as system has recently been revived by the structuralist interest in the work of Saussure. For the (Saussurean) structuralist sees language as a network of relationships in which each unit for analysis must be seen alongside those which contrast with it.[4] This works on every level, from that of phonology where 'pit' contrasts with 'bit', 'fit', 'kit', and so on, up to that of the lexical structures within language which may be exploited by the text. At this level, different texts (and the languages of which they are a part) can be seen to systematize different sets of relationships (like the possible meanings of books or physical actions). However, the problems we have in translating from one language to another can show that such sets are not necessarily isomorphic with one another across languages. Thus if we translate 'The cat sat on the mat' into French, we have to choose between 'être assis' and 's'asseoir' and to choose the type of mat—'paillasson', 'descente de lit', or 'tapis'. The potential importance of these rather dull semantic facts may be seen if we reflect on the fact that just as translation may exploit different lexical boundaries from that of its original text, so also will any interpretation of the text, which puts it into 'other words' within its *own* language. This will involve, on Saussurean principles, our moving into a different but related lexical system, from which we may select items, like those of 'dispraise of books'.

These potentially shifting selections are, as we write and as we interpret, made in two dimensions, according to Saussure.[5] The first is the syntagmatic, which combines elements on the same level, for example that of words, as in 'The tired author' (which is one of the set of forms Article+adjective+noun). It is at the syntagmatic level that we look for the syntactic rules of combination in a language, which may lead to linguistic patterning within a text, as in Cummings's repeated and finally disrupted formula (syntagm) of 'with a——around we——'. More interesting, from the interpretative point of view, is the complementary principle of selection which is the paradigmatic. Thus within any syntagmatic series, other units are substitutable, saving the syntagm but changing the paradigm—our author could thus be 'bored' or 'industrious', and these adjectives could in turn be applied to other nouns such as 'woman' or 'king', provided that such nouns are animate and human, and thus fit paradigmatically with 'psychological' adjectives. Thus in the Cummings example the final blank of the formula cited above is variously filled in with 'go yes'/'come who/'again fly'/'go all', and finally, 'we're alive'.

These rather simple observations seem to offer the prospect of a pleasing rigour and certainty : but matters become much more obscure when this very simple model for the organization of semantic fields within the language as a whole (the Saussurean 'langue') comes to the analysis of particular types of use (Saussurean 'parole'). For it is very difficult to discern the boundaries within which such lexical systems and their rules for substition or variation might operate in particular cases. For all texts subdivide on rather different principles.

Indeed the distinctions which such lexical systems encode seem to have some interesting and often perplexing properties. The first I wish to emphasize is that of *cultural salience*.[6] (This corresponds to what we said earlier about frameworks, to the exploitation by metaphor of culturally acceptable grounds of likeness, and to the organizing properties of our preferred metaphorical models). We make the distinctions we need within the culture and the environment in which we find ourselves in any historical period. That is why the Eskimos have so many words for snow, why English has a covert gender system which is at present being reorganized a little by the insertion of 'Ms' between 'Mrs' and 'Miss', and why Cummings may compare being in love to variously happy types of unimpeded physical activity.[7] The lexical structure of the language within texts thus reflects distinctions which are or have been important within the culture : Americans talk about the differences between Republicans and Democrats with a certain ease, and the natives of North Borneo do not (though they may well speak of the differences between their gods with an equal virtuosity). George Eliot can make the psychological world she projects seem to depend a great deal upon distinctions between different sorts of egoism, as opposed to imaginative sympathy. She thus makes distinctions within that family of moral concepts which runs through selfishness, self-interest, and altruism, to duty. This is of course a critic's interpretative family of concepts. We find when we look closer at the actual words she uses that they are rather different, though we do discover a systematic moral vocabulary.[8]

These culturally salient lexical structures are seen by many linguists as composed of semantic fields, and many structuralist theorists have urged that the structure of the text is in some respects isomorphic, with respect to the contrasts of Saussurean theory, to the semantic field/paradigm model. This is a notion which has a considerable importance for literature. Those structuralists who saw all texts as an example of an underlying 'science of the conditions of content',[9] and those interpreters who wish to demonstrate the underlying linguistic coherence of the text, or the way in which its is traversed by 'codes', all implicitly appeal to this notion.

The interpreter's notion of a code is thus from a linguistic point of view distinct from that of a variety of language, as in idiolect or register. The code is, for Hasan and others, above the linguistic system at the semiotic or 'social' level: 'the semantic properties of the codes can be predicted from the elements of social structure which in fact give rise to them. This raises the concept of 'code' to a more general level than that of language variety'.[10]

In our terms, codes are always seen as having cultural salience, whether as part of a text or as part of those codes of everyday life analysed by Bernstein and others: 'hence the codes transmit, or control the transmission of, the underlying patterns of a culture or sub-culture, acting through the socialising agencies of family, peer group and school.'[11] We learn our culture through its codes and also its interpretative methods, operative in our case within the sub-culture of academic interpretation. The code within the text can thus be defined as a semantic field which is given a social or ideological interpretation. Such codes, however, although they make a great appeal to our linguistic intuition, are not much susceptible of any rigorous demonstration, except in obvious cases, like those of kinship terms or of the colour system.[12] The important point to grasp for our purposes is that such key concepts in any field of interest may form part of a linguistic family or field whose members are in some form of contrastive relationship (as Cummings exploits the similarity and contrast between running, skipping, and so on). Hence Saussure's metaphor of language as dividing up an area: 'Dans l'intérieur d'une même langue, tous les mots qui expriment des idées voisines se limitent réciproquement: des synonymes comme redouter, craindre, avoir peur, n'ont de valeur propre que par leur opposition; si redouter n'existait pas, tout son contenu irait à ses concurrents.'[13]

The mature native speaker may be supposed to have some control over such interrelated concepts[14] and any reasonably extended text will have or imply systematic linguistic features which will as we have seen, themselves ultimately fit into a conceptual framework.

The Saussurean approach to the text thus leads us to concentrate upon its unification by semantic fields, which are often supposed to 'pre-exist' as part of our means of organizing language in our heads, but which can more typically and more importantly be brought to consciousness by the critic's exposition, through which we recognize the existence of a semantic field or code. We may also be given a more detailed insight into its cultural saliency or ideological implications. It is sometimes very difficult to distinguish between these two states of the code, as 'psychological' and as interpretative. For example, when the critic, for ideological reasons as we shall see, wishes to expose the prevalence of 'bourgeois' or 'authoritarian' or 'male chauvinist' codes in our thinking, he appeals to something that we are supposed to recognize was already there (a 'natural' way of thinking to us) but also makes us critically aware of this. He distances us from the interpretative distinctions we habitually make. I think that this odd balance between psychological shock of recognition and critical awareness exists in the best instances of this type of interpretation, which we will exemplify fully later.

Of course the semantic fields or codes we appealed to in discussing Cummings are hardly so controversial, and their presence allows us at least to say that the literary text is grammatically unified, as it clearly relies upon syntactic (syntagmatic) repetition, as well as on an organization of the (paradigmatic) semantic fields of its subject-matter. It thus plays upon our linguistic skills at quite a deep level. We need to be able to explain this if we are to show how we understand any peculiarly literary nature the text may have, and thus advance upon the logical notions of intelligibility advocated in our discussion of the salesman passage (pp. 4 ff.).

Structuralism in its early phase most explicitly took up this challenge, since it took (a usually Saussurean) linguistic model for all types of cultural analysis.[15] Structuralists of this period took the structures the critic discerned as being elements in the constitutive literary 'rules' governing the text being investigated. Thus Culler once roundly asserted that 'The cultural meaning of any particular act or object is determined by a whole [Saussurean] system of constitutive rules : rules which do not regulate behaviour so much as create the possibility of certain forms of behaviour.'[16]

As applied to the literary text, this approach reveals 'a desire to isolate codes, to name their various languages, with and among which the text plays, to go beyond manifest content to a series of forms, and then to make these forms or oppositions a model of signification, the burden of the text.'[17] Thus in the Cummings poem we have an opposition between the 'book' code and the 'physical action' code, which have a contrastive relationship which is deeply embedded in our culture, and thus expresses a mimetic commitment which (paradoxically for a poet) sees being bookish and being physically active as likely to be opposed, and which thus implicitly likens being in love to physical action (like Paolo and Francesca, giving up reading for something more immediately engaging). But this is pretty obvious stuff: and what advance have we (yet) made by appealing to codes here? (As opposed for example to the associated commonplaces noted for metaphor.) We have opposed as linguistic codes what earlier critics were willing to call themes.[18] Both modes of expression rely upon well-embedded critical assumptions, but the structuralist seemed to place the meaning of the poem within the language, rather than within the associative powers or the common knowledge of the reader.[19]

There are it seems two interrelated areas worth attention as they involve themselves in this kind of linguistically sensitive reading:

(1) Our awareness of the way in which fields or codes are brought into play by (or in conflict with) the sequence of our attention to the text, and

(2) Our awareness of cohesion or coherence-conferring linguistic features of the text, which may derive from the codes it implies or activates.

This is an important matter for interpretative judgment, for as Kuhns remarks, 'interdependence as a textual relationship is far more variable—and generally far weaker—than it is in a logical system. Yet the articulation of precisely what kind of interdependence obtains in a given text is a prime obligation of ours in reading it, for reading requires choosing the boundaries within which the text will be explicated'.[20]

The problems raised by the first of these were discussed in the opening section : the considerations urged there can, I think, be seen to apply to almost any use of language, even if they become most interesting and complex when applied to literary narrative.[21] I wish to argue in what follows that the second type of attention to the text seems to demand conventions of reading and interpretation which are perhaps peculiar to literature. The ability to perceive cohesion seems to require a competence which is typically taught to the reader by the critic, and by critics to each other. And yet it is very difficult indeed to draw a clear line between the basic requirements for the intelligibility of any text, which we discussed at the outset, and those special literary conventions that help make literary texts meaningful.

For ordinary utilitarian prose about car salesmen obviously does not call for that type of structural juxtaposition we sketched for Cummings. This awareness of juxtaposition or parallelism does seem to be particularly demanded by works of art, and using it in the service of interpretation to be a particular type of skill. Culler and others have suggested 'literary competence' as the name for our grasping of these special literary conventions—thus acquiring a skill which makes reading poetry 'a rule-governed process of producing meanings'. But there are difficulties with such a notion. We already have ample reason to doubt that literary competence could be purely linguistic or conventionally rule-governed, and so the term itself may be misleading, coming as it does from Chomsky, who uses it to describe a general linguistic ability of all native speakers. Literary competence in fact seems to be taught as part of the educational process and the meanings it produces may depend upon quite specialized literary conventions, so that certainty in interpretation is most unlikely to be guaranteed by any such 'rules'.[23]

The sophisticated reader is instantaneously master of a complex family of such conventions. That is why the unpacking moves of theoretical analysis often seem so clumsy. They make explicit what we manage to do without conscious effort in the act of reading.

There are then two types of competence involved in our dealings with the literary text, and although they may be distinguished in theory, they are inextricably tangled together in fact. The first is the basic Chomskyan linguistic competence which runs from the most literal to the most metaphorical uses of language: we have been concerned with aspects of this in our first two sections. The second is a more specifically literary competence, more specific because it deals with what in a particular historical context may be thought of as literary, e.g. generic, conventions. The critic helps to create a set of conventions which stabilize the interpretation of particular types of literary text. However as we shall see such conventions are liable to change. One of the most important of these conventions to which we have already made reference, puts these two types of competence into conflict and overrides the first in favour of the second. For on second reading we may revise our purely sequential reading of a text in favour of a supplementary juxtapository one : when we see, for example, that stanza is *like* stanza in certain thematic respects.

However, the description of such conventions may not be thought to be part of interpretation proper, but an analysis of the conditions for it. This is an argument put by Barthes, with which I agree. For when the early structuralists saw texts as systems of signs to be studied by 'poetics' as linguists studied language, they treated them as exemplary manifestations of an underlying system, whose conventions must be revealed. These conventions make the meanings we negotiate in interpretation possible. This 'science of the conditions of content' in Barthes's phrase, may thus be thought of as prior to interpretation.[24] The construction of a poetics is thus a form of description, and we have then to be able to distinguish between such descriptions as are merely so to speak technical, and those which are critically useful for interpretation in any given case. This difference, which it is impossible to make completely rigid, can be made at least intuitively clear by considering the following two answers, both of which are true; but the second is certainly more useful to someone wanting to use a car rather than have a banal and inevitably selective structural description of it :

It has two seats in the front and two at the back and windows all round and four wheels.

It will do 42 m.p.g., has a roomy driver's seat, quick acceleration, and room in the back for four suitcases.

Correspondingly, I argue that the interpretative statement should tell us, not what the linguistic structure of the text is, but what it can mean within a reading, which can form the basic for all sorts of uses. (One might say that linguistic features have to be shown to serve the purposes of a rhetoric.) But these distinctions need an example to make them clearer.

3.2 'Leda and the Swan' : Three Approaches

A sudden blow : the great wings beating still
Above the staggering girl, her thighs caressed
By the dark webs, her nape caught in his bill
He holds her helpless breast upon his breast.

How can those terrified vague fingers push
The feathered glory from her loosening thighs?
And how can body, laid in that white rush,
But feel the strange heart beating where it lies?

A shudder in the loins engenders there
The broken wall, the burning roof and tower
And Agamemnon dead.

                  Being so caught up,
So mastered by the brute blood of the air,
Did she put on his knowledge with his power
Before the indifferent beak could let her drop?

M. A. K. Halliday attempts a linguistic description of parts of this poem.[1] He is interested in the main in two of its features : its use of 'the' and the distribution of its verbal items. The latter will perhaps make the contrast between linguistic descriptions and interpretations of the text most strikingly. Halliday says : 'most of this poem, especially the first ten and a half lines, is organised in nominal groups; they account for 69 of the 83 words in this first part. There are 15 verbal groups in this poem, and in addition four words of the class 'verb' operating directly in the structure (as opposed to being rankshifted into) nominal groups ('staggering', 'loosening', 'burning', 'broken').' He then gives a table of these verbal groups, showing that if they are ranked on a scale from the most 'verbish' of all, the finite verbal group in free clause, to the most attenuated, 'subordinated altogether to the nominal element without even the formality of a rankshift', then 'Leda', compared to samples from 'His Phoenix' and *Morte d'Arthur*, has a 'preponderance of nominal groups' so that its 'verbal items are considerably deverbalised'. Halliday remarks that 'Of various short passages examined for comparative purposes, the only one showing a distribution at all comparable to that of *Leda* was a passage of prose from the *New Scientist* concerning the peaceful uses of plutonium'.[2] It is only when Halliday goes on to write of the 'lexical power' of these verbs that he seems to come near to an interpretation of the meaning of the poem, as one concerning rape:

> In 'Leda' the few verbal items are varied in power, though medium rather than extreme. But they get lexically more powerful as they get grammatically less 'verbal' : in finite verbal group in free clause we have 'hold', 'push', 'put on', 'feel' ; while at the other end of the scale, including some not operating in verbal group at all, are 'stagger', 'loosen' and 'caress'.
>
> Lexical power is the measure of the restriction on high probability collocations : the fewer the items with which a given item is likely to collocate (put another way, the more strongly the item tends to be associated with other items) the more 'powerful' it is said to be.[3]

We are left with the feeling that Halliday's comparisons of 'Leda' with other texts, while no doubt descriptively adequate within linguistic theory, offer few or no clues as to the way in which the poem should be interpreted. Nor, particularly in view of his remark that 'Leda' is like the *New Scientist*, need we suspect that Halliday is analysing the underlying linguistic structure of a literary convention, as earlier defined. Indeed he makes it clear that to do this we would have to analyse something quite different—the rhetorical functions (what is 'effective') of different registers.[4] It is in any case impossible to imagine any convention (or 'rule' in Culler's terms) that could govern two such disparate passages. Nor I think would a rhetoric have much to say about this particular type of use of verbs.[5]

In our terms, Halliday's analysis deliberately draws back from specifying an interpretative significance for the features he has discerned in the text. Another mode of analysis which purports to come much closer to the construction of a 'poétique', i.e. to purely literary conventions (which would not, one presumes, be found in the *New Scientist*) is that of Roman Jakobson.[6] Here distributional analyses of pattern within literary texts are supposedly correlated with what I have called rhetorical or poetic functions. (For example when Jakobson points out that 'I like Ike' deploys a high degree of phonetic repetition, whose function is to present a 'paronomastic image of the loving subject enveloped by the beloved object'.[7]) But what will constrain our choice of these distributive categories—descriptive linguistic or rhetorical affective considerations? If they are purely linguistic, then the relevance of description to interpretation is far from guaranteed, as we saw from Halliday; if not simply linguistic, then our choice of categories for analysis will very likely

derive from pre-existent assumptions concerning literary conventions. For as Jakobson wrote in 1919: 'the real field of literary science
is not literature but *literariness*: in other words, that which makes a
specific work literary.'[8]

The central objection to Jakobsonian method has been made by
Culler:

A complete grammar of a language will, of course, assign structural
description to every sentence, and if the grammar is explicit two analysts
using it will assign the same description to the given sentence; but once one
goes beyond this stage and undertakes a distributional analysis of a text, one
enters a realm of extraordinary freedom, where a grammar, however
explicit, no longer provides a determinant method . . . [the] process of
progressive differentiation can produce an almost unlimited number of
distributive classes, and thus if one wishes to discern a pattern of symmetry
in a text, one can always produce some class whose members will be
appropriately arrayed.[9]

It is in the light of this sort of objection that the Jakobson claim to be
applying methods of linguistics mechanically, without bias, begins
to look a little suspect. The method reveals linguistic structures
which are in some sense 'there', but it may well be then the function
of the interpretative critic to choose those structures to which he can
intelligibly assign a pragmatic rhetorical function.

Thus we might proceed in Jakobsonian fashion with respect to
'Leda' by first dividing the sonnet into 'stanzas' (4 + 4 + 3 + 3) and
then look to see if there is any symmetrical distribution of
grammatical items about these groups. This would be done in
pursuit of Jakobson's claim that in literary texts the principle of
equivalence is as important as that of sequence. Thus Jakobson
asserts, correctly in my view, that 'in poetry similarity is imposed on
contiguity, and hence equivalence is promoted to the constitutive
device of the sequence'.[10] I think this actually comes to saying, as I
have earlier, that structural juxtapositions are as important for
literary interpretation as logical sequence.

If we look then for a symmetrical, juxtapository distribution in
'Leda' we might look at pronominal forms, which are distributed as
follows;

   I: her, he, her, his
  II: her
 III: (there)
 IV: she, his, her

It is difficult to get any interpretative significance out of this pattern
as a whole, except to point out that in the absence of pronominal
forms in III, when the poem makes an impersonal reflection, the

'there' comes to seem to be an ambiguous term for 'her' ('there = 'in her') if we try to assimilate the mode of III to that of I, II, and IV. But this is not much of a result, and its significance depends as we shall later see, on a much more complex apparatus of interpretation.

Similarly, if we follow up Jakobson's insistence that rhyme is not mere phonological repetition but may express a semantic relationship[11] of similarity or dissimilarity of meaning we find:

      I: still/bill, caressed/breast
     II: push/rush, thighs/lies
III/IV: there/air, tower/power, up/drop

These couplings may indeed be made significant—but not, I think as isolated linguistic features. It is only in the context of the interpretation of the poem as a whole that the correlation of 'tower' and 'power' for example might become significant, though why one should derive this from a comparison of rhyme words rather than from a sequential analysis is to me very obscure. But under these conditions, the claim to reveal significant features of a poem by the 'objective' means of linguistic description alone has to be given up. And in any case the features we have isolated are not in themselves likely to reveal any significant literary convention (except that of rhyme, which we knew about before we read); any more than did those analysed by Halliday. What is missing so far is any plausible relationship between linguistic form and the reader's response, and this, as we have argued from the outset, is wholly dependent upon the reader's constructing a context and co-text of situation for the text as a whole—dependent that is, upon the deployment of non-linguistic knowledge.

Suppose then we look at this psychological process as it is structured by the work of art, and controlled to a very high degree by its rhetoric. As we would expect, the text requires an effort at the comprehension of truths internal to the text (co-textual implications concerning the situation it projects) which raise an interest in its own outcome, and leave us to anticipate certain of its aspects.

In the following analysis I am concerned both with what I shall call the primary sequence of reading, and also with some secondary reflections upon linguistic patterns in the poem (these correspond to the distinction made earlier between sequence and cohesion in our reading). These two processes are in subordination to one another, for the juxtapository structures discerned in secondary reflection can only be the result of scanning back through the sequence.

LEDA AND THE SWAN

The title will call up as between speaker and hearer varying amounts of knowledge concerning the subject of the poem. It is impossible to specify the depth of this background, which, as we have seen, it is often the critic's task to augment, and which would in various ways affect our reading. The main point concerning the title is that it will supply a framework-hypothesis concerning the subject of the poem, to be confirmed or disconfirmed by the schema development of what follows.[12] This frame will probably centre, if the reader knows of the myth, upon the sexual relationship of a mortal and a god in the guise of an animal. Thus

> A sudden blow:

leads us to ask: where are we in the causal sequence of the story? How can we begin to construct its situation? The opening produces an appropriately sudden disequilibrium in the reader's mental set, which is stabilized by what follows

> the great wings beating still,
> Above the staggering girl, her thighs caressed
> By the dark webs, her nape caught in his bill
> He holds her helpless breast upon his breast.

We thus construct a scene of rape, evoking a sexual response, a composition of bird and woman in a picture which begins in action and then becomes passive and static. Hence perhaps the paradoxical contradiction of 'beating still' (though I may be overinfluenced here by the analogies drawn by the critics between this poem and its iconographic parallels). This is an impression reinforced on the secondary level by the simple completed 'action' of the quatrain scheme (*a b a b*) and the blank space paragraphing of the poem. But this remark depends upon a literary convention which really appeals to an analogy—we may say that a rhetorically enclosed rhyming stanza is 'complete' in the way that an action leading to stasis is 'complete'. The literary structure becomes a metaphor for its fictional situation. A willingness to respond to this appeal could only I think be the product of a literary competence, which is essentially taught by remarks such as the preceding ones. The poem continues

> How can those terrified vague fingers push
> The feathered glory from her loosening thighs?
> And how can body, laid in that white rush,
> But feel the strange heart beating where it lies?

This is Leda's position, which, upon reflection, we see as antithetically represented in an answering quatrain. The situation has been

re-described, but the rhetorical mode, and the corresponding
relationship between speaker and hearer, has changed from assertion to questioning, so that we now need answers which are not
obviously supplied by the poet's subsequent assertions.

> A shudder in the loins

(his and hers)

> engenders there

(something, both at that time, and in her womb). We may well feel a
sexual parallelism here between 'strange heart beating' and the
'shudder in the loins' so that the strange heart is a displaced or
periphrastic image for the penis. But the action has also moved on,
with the sense of futurity in 'engenders' to

> The broken wall, the burning roof and tower
> And Agamemnon dead.

Here a verb which seems to demand an animate and human object
turns out to have inanimate ones, and so at this point we have an
immediate problem concerning relevance or pragmatic implication.
How can these two lines be implied by the preceding one? We must
supply additional premisses that will secure relevance by adverting
to the larger situation as we know it from myth. We use our
knowledge of the histories of Leda's children, who were Helen,
Castor, and Polydeuces (and in some versions Clytemnaestra,
for Leda was subsequently deified as Nemesis.) 'From one of the
eggs came love, from the other, war'. The causal implications of
'engender' are metaphorically extended to include not simply the
biological but also the historical consequences of the birth of Helen
from one of Leda's eggs and the Trojan War.

But there is a second type of relevance here, which may lead us to
accept a metaphorical interpretation of these lines based on sexual
symbolism, which will help indeed to preserve a thematic unity in
the poem. It will in any case be there subconsciously, if Freud and
his followers are right. For we are so far involved in sexual imagery
that it is hard to avoid a sexual connotation. What is 'there' may
thus be interpreted as the sexual organs in the disguises of the tower-
like penis, the broken wall of the hymen, and the burning roof of the
vagina penetrated by the penis. I use the word 'like' here designedly,
for what is at issue in this type of interpretation is the process of
metaphor, which has to be grounded by referential elements of
likeness which in Freudian cases are often surprisingly general, as

between any upright penetrative object and any enclosing one. The truth conditions for this type of paraphrase are of course interestingly problematic, as they depend in turn on the truth of the supporting Freudian theory.

  After this

                    Being so caught up,

        So mastered

recapitulates the verbs for the rape so far, as 'blow', 'beating', 'staggering', 'caressed', 'caught', 'holds her helpless', 'terrified', 'push', 'loosening', 'laid', 'beating', 'lies', 'feel', 'shudder', 'broken', 'burning', 'dead'. Note the way in which these have a causal order even out of context, their number showing Yeats's minute attention to the process of action here. Leda is mastered

            by the brute blood of the air

which gives us a personifying and terrifying periphrasis for the swan, rhetorically metamorphosed as Zeus is in the myth. This subtle linguistic change moves us, appropriately, into further abstract thinking.

        Did she put on his knowledge with his power?

Is another question, to which we are challenged to find an answer (but also an implicit reply to 'And how can body . . . lies?'). It is a puzzling question with its use of the anomalous verb 'put on', which suggests clothing, and it is also paradoxical that the sequence should conclude 'put on his knowledge' since he in the Biblical sense had knowledge of her,

        Before the indifferent beak could let her drop?

We have closure in the completed actions of the swan, and the poem, from 'sudden blow' to 'drop' (single and enclosed like the sonnet form). We have a possible answer to lines 5 and 8 and a final third question. At this point we are thus urged by Yeats to go beyond the poem and to reflect on the significance and consequences of an action. The answer may be 'no', or 'I do not know', but this is unsatisfying and we are strongly pushed towards 'yes'. If this is the answer, then we may infer, by using interpretative strategies which allow us now to see the poem as a whole, what important knowledge Leda acquired. This was indeed the knowledge of god-like power, 'brute blood of the air', but possibly also god-like foreknowledge, of 'The broken wall the burning roof and tower,/And Agamemnon dead', in its historical sense. For if we see the poem with Yeats's historical system in mind, as an annunciation parallel to that made by the winged Angel to Mary, then we ask quasi-theological questions of the kind raised by Christian theologians. Did Mary have full knowledge of her son's ultimate fate? (This would make 'Leda' worth comparing to 'The Mother of God' in the *Collected Poems*, 281), which includes the lines 'The terror of all terrors that I bore/The Heavens in my womb'). Leda's shudder is orgasmic but also fearful.

This would provide an elegant solution to our problem. We are satisfied if we have by abstraction (and perhaps only temporarily) ordered the complexities of the poem, in order to answer its questions, which urge interpretation upon us. We need a solution because of the intense dramatic import of the poem, and the antithesis in its illocutionary realization between statement and question. All poems, as complex and inherently problematic uses of language, force us to make some such effort after meaning; this one is unusual in that it asks us to do so explicitly.

Some of the secondary reflections I have noted, e.g. the pattern of violent verbs and past participles performing similar functions, may be subconsciously present in our primary reading and thus contribute to our unified affective response (though this would presuppose that coherence-conferring semantic fields could be correlated with emotions). The main burden of our interpretation thus depends upon a balance between an internalized mode of meaning, and the situationally based mode that we discussed at the outset, as they apply to the central codes within the poem. They might be called a Rape Code, which also includes a Body Code

    staggering; thigh; nape; breast/fingers (push) (loosening)
    thighs; body//loins// (she?) her drop (i.e. her body drop)
which is logically controlled by the pattern of pronouns we looked at earlier.

This balance comes into play when we see the codes not simply as sequences enacting a situation in a dramatically logical order, but as interrelated in a unifying way with the poem. They thus have a double aspect; they represent a selection within a paradigm which unifies the poem, but they also express a specifiable type of cultural salience. For once we look at the diction of the poem as a whole we can see that the codes involve choices within a paradigm system of some cultural significance. We may for example in comparing Yeats's selection with the generally available codes for rape ask why he chooses in the body-code words like 'nape' and 'loins', makes 'breast' ambiguous, and so on. We notice that these are largely 'poetic', indirect, periphrastic words (though the loosening of the thighs is direct enough) which distance, and dignify his account. This periphrastic mode becomes of course most dramatically obvious at the climax of the sexual act and of the poem, where the text veers away into a not obviously relevant historical remark whose sexual implications have to be mediated through metaphor. This periphrastic mode indeed runs right through the poem as synecdoche perpetually forces us to supply an unwritten sense ('feathered glory', 'white rush', 'a shudder in the loins', 'brute blood of the air'). As Hartman points out 'these non-naming figures have the structure of riddles as well as of descriptions'.[13] The codes thus unify the poem as a semantic field related to the body, but they also make us interpret it as indirectly related to the situation when we ask 'what is really going on?' They also depend upon a further master code with a considerable history, as can be seen from many sonnet sequences—that of making an act of war equivalent to an act of sex. This code leads back into the more generally pervasive metaphorical models within ordinary language which link sex with aggression.

However it should be remembered that our interpretation of 'Leda' has taken us a long way beyond the explanation of its language and of the patterns into which it falls. Indeed its implications, in all the senses which we have so far given the term, naturally form the major part of the interpretation, since the critic—interpreter is only necessary in so far as he supplements the text. We thus made explicit the co-textual situation within the poem, that of rape, and showed that the consequences of this in turn depended upon the 'encyclopaedia' or the framework of belief. In this case, principally the myth which leads from the swan as Zeus, through Leda to Helen and war in Troy. We also noted that there may be an implied parallel sequence: Angel/Holy Ghost/Mary/Jesus/Crucifixion. But if we consider an interpretation as far-fetched as this, we must realize that we have gone beyond the text, to place it in its own context of situation as a poem communicated by a speculative poet to an audience, who also performs through his discourse the roles of questioner, doubter, visionary, etc., and who can expect us to exploit our knowledge of a parallel historical situation. Yeats's stance is one that Geoffrey Hartman for one is inclined to question: 'Where got Yeats that truth? Part of the magic to be resisted is the poet's imperious assumption of a visionary mode, as if it were self-justifying. His exotic and erotic subject matter displaces the question of authority. For Yeats may be a voyeur rather than a visionary . . .'[14]

4 The Text and the External World

It is by words and the defeat of words,
Down sudden vistas of the vain attempt,
That for a flying moment we may see
By what cross purposes the world is dreamt.

Richard Wilbur, 'An Event'

I have so far used the notion of 'situation', which is crucial to interpretation, in an ambiguous manner. All texts, I argue, construct situations which control a great deal of what it is plausible to say in interpretations. Any attempt to establish a semantic pattern within a text (of the kind involved in talk of codes and metaphorical models) is only plausible if we are aware of its relation to such possible states of affairs, for as Culler remarks, 'we may interpret statements about the weather as metaphors for states of mind, but no one ever read statements about moods as metaphors for the weather.'[1] These situations are part of the mimetic commitments of the text. They thus relate to the ways in which we think about the world, via the encyclopaedia, and our sense of the cultural salience of the codes which the text contains. The notion of mimetic commitment here is supposed to indicate the fact that all texts implicitly select an area of experience with which to deal. Thus as Iris Murdoch points out with respect to Ryle's *Concept of Mind*: it reflects 'the world in which people play cricket, cook cakes, make simple decisions, remember their childhood and go to the circus, not the world in which they commit sins, fall in love, say prayers or join the Communist party.'[2]

My argument so far has tended to show that the text is in a potential if problematic relationship to the external world, or at least to what we take as the framework of our knowledge and belief about it. But there is of course a further question, which we have touched on already in discussing the fictional and historical features of the Rumelhart example (pp. 7 ff.), and also in our discussion of the interpretative paraphrase of metaphor. Do we, in interpreting the text, take the relationship between it and the world outside it as actually or potentially referential?

The philosopher's notion of reference is a complicated one in which the relation of reference is usually taken to hold between an expression and some other really existent portion of reality, whether anyone knows it or not. We can thus only be certain of reference when we are also certain of what exists in fact. A more liberal view based on intention will allow us to refer to, at least in the sense of 'talk about', both existent and non-existent objects or persons such as London and Sherlock Holmes. The battle between the two views is at least partly terminological. In what follows I shall take reference to be a relationship, intended or not, between a linguistic text and objects, persons, actions, or events which we as interpreters suppose to exist or have existed in history, outside the text. (Reference in this sense typically picks out or identifies particulars.)

The tendency of much recent criticism, influenced as it has been by the Saussurean model of language as a self-enclosed system, has been to deny that any such references are actual, let alone necessary for interpretation. We are given the impression that it is possible to investigate the language of the text from the 'inside' without any concern for reference or mimesis :

A language . . . does not construct its formations of words by reference to the patterns of 'reality' but on the basis of its own internal and self sufficient rules. The word 'dog' exists, and functions within the structures of the English language, without reference to any four-legged barking creature's real existence. The word's behaviour derives from its inherent structural status as a noun rather than its referent's actual status as an animal. Structures are characteristically closed in this way.[3]

This hostility to the mimetic function of literature as traditionally conceived, stems largely from the Derridan redevelopment of Saussure—the conception of the text as a 'play' amongst 'differences' within language, rather than as reflecting reality. We will discuss such claims fully at a later stage. I am concerned here to see what can be said for the mimetic view, that is for the way in which we 'naturalize' a text. This operation is at its most overt perhaps, when we feel we have to choose between a naturalizing or a supernatural or fantastic interpretation of the text's events.[4] We try to situate the text in a world acceptable to ourselves (in terms of what 'really exists') by constructing for it a context which will make even the apparently absurd (Beckett, surrealism) meaningful. We are more often involved, of course with a more modest interpretative strategy, that of the *'vraisemblable'*: 'One can speak of the vraisemblance of a work in so far as it attempts to make us believe that it conforms to reality and not to its own laws. In other words the vraisemblable is the mask which conceals the text's own laws and which we are supposed to take for a relation with reality.'[5] In making this relationship, we do not necessarily make a direct correspondence between the text and external reality (using it like a map). We more likely match two types of discourse, that of the text, and that which we use as interpreters.

I wish to test this sort of view, by looking at the interpretation by Riffaterre of Wordsworth's 'Yew Trees', an interpretation which is specifically designed to attack what is called the 'referential fallacy'.[6] Riffaterre argues that 'the representation of reality is a verbal construct in which meaning is achieved by reference from words to words not things', and further that 'the verbal process whereby . . . significance is actually perceived when the poem is read . . . can best be understood as an awareness of verbal structure rather than in terms of referentiality' (230).

The status of this remark as a recommendation as to how we should read and interpret is revealed by the significant word 'best'. Riffaterre wishes us to place the poem, not in a pragmatic relationship to external reality, its context in our sense, but as somehow self-contained. His recommendation appears to have a severe test with reference to 'Yew Trees', because the poem does indeed make a specific reference:

> There is a Yew-Tree, pride of Lorton Vale,
> Which to this day stands single . . .

and as Riffaterre points out, 'literary pilgrims have verified it on the spot . . . We also know that Wordsworth changed certain facts about these yews because they did not suit his purpose' (231). He goes on, quite correctly in my view, to make the point that 'The locus of the literary phenomenon is limited to the text–reader relationship which includes such reactions as a belief in its likeness to reality' (231).

This seems to be all that a referential theory of literature might require; that is, it is not necessary to believe in the relationship of the words to actual trees (for our reading of the poem, the literary pilgrims' activities are unnecessary). Our interpretation of the poem does not turn on our comparison of the text to the world *in these particular respects*, however independently interesting the facts concerning such a correspondence or lack of it may be. But it will, as I shall argue, turn on a notion of likeness.

Riffaterre also goes on to point out, correctly I believe, that the reference to a specific vale is also strictly speaking unnecessary—a general concept of a vale is all that we require. Again I would point out that this requirement, of the correct general concept, is also a fairly strong one; to think that Lorton Vale was like the Grand Canyon would not do. However Riffaterre is I think wrong when he goes on to argue that *all* information of this (specific, or proper name) kind in the poem can be similarly generalized. He says:

'"drew their sounding bows" suffices to make "Azincour" a battle, and "bows" suffices to set it back in the depths of the middle ages. The argument that everyone knows about Agincourt is irrelevant: how long will people still know? And when Agincourt has disappeared from the reader's mythology, will the text be less evocative? Certainly not . . .' (232). The answer is that it *will* be less evocative. And this cannot be obscured by the sleight of hand of Riffaterre's reference to historical knowledge as 'mythology'. A critic who is willing to make this move isn't just sloppily sceptical about history: he is willing to allow readers to become ignorant of it. For there are certain facts about Agincourt (for example, that it was a British victory over the French) which indeed makes the poem more 'evocative': and what is more, because of this, it licenses Wordsworth's praise of the tree as 'not loth to furnish weapons' for those who 'drew their sounding bows at Azincour'. (Suppose the battle had been a defeat for the English, like Hastings.) The poem can of course be understood on some basic level by the ignorant reader: but it is undoubtedly the case that it carries more implications which can be shown to be relevant for particular purposes, for the knowledgeable one, and no theoretical manœuvrings can disguise this fact. For what is at issue is the evaluative matter of the interpreter's attitude to history. Poets may indeed expect us to possess certain factual and literary knowledge (think of *The Waste Land*) even if some critics may view its disappearance with equanimity. It is thus absurdly wrong, though alas typical, for Riffaterre to place literature above history, and allow it to reduce it to a 'phantasm' when he says that 'Associations here do not work from outside history to the text, but the other way round. The text builds up a phantasm of history' (232). The chicken-and-egg argument of the first sentence could hardly apply to Wordsworth's original intentions or to the reaction of the informed reader. The implication of the second sentence is that we should prefer fiction or fantasy to fact, which is a position which cannot be sustained to its logical end, since it would end up by preferring ignorance to knowledge, and myth to history.

Riffaterre appears to be partly wrong then, at least in his account of this type of factual reference. How then does his second line of argument, which asserts that we would better be aware of verbal structures rather than of history, fare? He is really trying I think, not so much to free poetry of its historical context as to define literariness as a form of linguistic self-containment, as did the theorists cited earlier. Thus he argues, that even were it possible, 'one to one referentiality would not suffice per se to turn a truthful account of nature into a literary text . . . it would not endow a recording of reality with literariness' (234). Now this is again a persuasive definition with hidden evaluative premisses. For according to Riffaterre, although each word of the text may seem to refer to a particular detail, it is better seen as part of a unified semantic field or code (and it is the latter property which counts as 'literary'). We see this in his dealings with lines 16 to 18, for example:

> 'Huge trunks!—and each particular trunk a growth
> Of intertwisted fibres serpentine
> Up-coiling, and inveterately convolved,—

What actually happens in this sentence is that adjectives and participles all spring from one word. They do seem to progress, as a description should, from feature to feature of the trunk. But being synonyms, they actually repeat the same meaning through a modulation from code to code. First we have a wood code, or living-matter code, represented by 'intertwisted fibres'. 'Intertwisted' not so much adds to 'fibre' as it activates and singles out the most important feature in the semantic complex of 'fibre'. That is to say, 'fibre' as a part of an organic, living fabric, 'fibre' as a component incapable of independent existence (except under autopsy) tied to other fibres by something that is not mere contiguity or technical function, for that would be mineral or metallic or artificial. 'Fibre' as bound to other fibres by links complex enough, and labyrinthine enough, to become a kind of image within an image of the complexity of life. Hence 'intertwisted'. But then 'serpentine' takes up 'intertwisted' by a variation or transformation into 'snake code'. All the more effective because many stereotypes do describe vegetable life in terms of slow, crawling progress, like vines creeping up tree trunks or walls—that is, reptilian terms. 'Up-coiling' confirms the snake code, but brings it back closer to the verticality characteristic of vegetable life and this confirms also the image of the tree as a striving upwards through centuries. 'Inveterately convolved' summarises what precedes. Now all these details are but a grammatical expansion of the meaning of the word 'growth' which is in itself only a generalisation of 'trunk' (234).

What Riffaterre does here is to show, though he uses the language of the code, something that we have already noticed in metaphor and in our analysis of 'Leda'; the passage systematically exploits a semantic field or system of associated commonplaces, or what he calls 'stereotypes'. In doing so it is semantically unified, with all that ambiguity we noticed before, between the psychological appeal to our powers of association as exemplified by the critic on the one hand, and the theoretical assumption that structures 'in the language' license them. The passage thus has, according to Riffaterre, a semantic common denominator: the word 'trunk' is described in words that all share (or connote metaphorically) the same characteristic—'complex irresistible mobility' (235). This is a very familiar version of the analytic unpacking of metaphor or symbol, within the model of the code. That is why I asserted earlier that this mode of analysis supports a coherence theory of the literary text. It sees the poem as a kind of tautological unpacking which displays language as already given: 'In a poem, the descriptive sentence is a chain of relations. Each word is generated by positive or negative conformity with the preceding one—that is either by synonymy or antonymy—and the sequence is thus tautological or oxymoronic . . . a tautological sequence enumerates some or most of the semantic features making up a kernel word' (235).[7]

As a method of analysis of the way language works in a poem, Riffaterre's observations here and elsewhere are often acceptable. They certainly lead to brilliantly detailed and suggestive analyses of particular texts. What are not so acceptable are the conclusions drawn from these analyses concerning the 'autonomy' of the language of the poem, without sufficient regard for its use within the world, and hence for the relationship of the poem to the external world surrounding it. For example when Riffaterre asserts that 'the description has verisimilitude because it in fact confirms again and again the same statements in various codes. The relationship of literary description to its subject matter is not a relationship of language to its own verbal contexts but that of metalanguage to language' (236). He relies on what is basically a Snark-like argument—what I tell you three times is true—and confuses, as a theory of truth, internal coherence or consistency with correspondence. And in making this sort of assertion Riffaterre thus suppresses or forgets the fact that the 'metalanguages' he appeals to could not have these inter-relationships unless the system as a whole had a relationship to the external world. For the language the poet uses is the very same language (it could not be otherwise) with which in purely referential contexts we may talk about trees or any other of the subjects of Wordsworth's poem. It is systematic, precisely because we divide up reality, not language, in a particular way. (Indeed what the Saussurean may forget is the historical reasons for the oppositions and distinctions he knows.) The language of the poem only counts as systematically related because it selects and develops features (of trees or anything else) that are taken to be systematically related in the external world. Its verisimilitude is thus essential to it in a very strong sense.

It would thus be quite wrong to say that the distinctions within this poem analysed by Riffaterre himself, for example those embedded in that part of the poem which he says is 'a transformation of the basic opposition, Nature versus Artefact' (236) (cf. lines 20–31 of the poem) are of no general importance for our grasp of the relation of the poem to our general beliefs about the world. Wordsworth's willingness to see the grove of trees as a natural temple does relate, contra Riffaterre, to precisely those 'norms of thought, or the conventions of society at a given time' which he blithely asserts 'interpretation does not need to know' (236). The attitude of the Romantics to this type of natural religion was quite distinctive, and has been of considerable historical and ideological importance. It would be a pity if a critical theory devoted to internal linguistic analysis had to deprive us of an awareness of this dimension of the poem's significance. Riffaterre is thus in my view simply wrong when he asserts that 'interpretation does not start with a judgement as to whether there is a consistency with a hypothetical consensus about reality. It starts with a judgement as to whether there is compatibility among the words distributed along the syntagm' (236). It has precisely to start with a reliance on consistency to reality because without such a consensus, any compatibility amongst the words of the description could not be perceived. It is thus false that 'the system's components and their combinatory rules are simply language level restrictions upon use' (238), for there can never be any simple language-level restrictions upon the use of descriptive terms.

Thus Riffaterre is not making any substantial point about the nature of the literary text, but about the way in which he would have us read and use it. Hence his use of the word 'fallacy' is improperly suggestive, for what is involved is not so much a logical mistake which all must avoid, as a perfectly intelligible mode of thinking about the text that he attacks.

In any case, I argue that general criteria for reference and description will still be operative, governing verisimilitude, where descriptions are non-specific. That is we have to know what yews, trees, temples, groves, and so on, are like in the real world in order to understand the poem. Thus mimesis (as an obedience to general conditions of reference and description) always operates independently of any specific reference to specific states of affairs. In particular it allows frames and schemata to be activated for concepts and thus includes our sense of 'what is likely to go together'.

The interpreter may make these conditions explicit, by mediating the relationship of the text to the world in terms of a general likeness relationship, where likeness is grounded (as it is in metaphor) by the respects which he may specify. Just as in the case of metaphor, the reader or interpreter selects these. The ultimate ground will lie in a judgement as to matters of fact, not of language. This is not of course to suggest that such facts are simply given. What counts as a fact, and the way it is described, may well ultimately depend on a quite complex series of assumptions. But it seems to me difficult to avoid the contention that some basic facts about the world are such that all reasonable men would accept them (for example, that Henry V fought at Agincourt). Difficulties arise for the interpreter when we rise above this level—and, indeed, make interpretations, which are complex constructions placed upon facts which, as all controversialists know, may at the same time be 'indubitable' and yet tendentiously selected.

In asserting the text's likeness to the world, I should make clear that I am concerned with the notion as it actually applies in acts of interpretation. Most theorists of world–text relationships have concerned themselves with matters of correspondence: what one can or cannot say about the actual relationship of text to world: to say, for example, that we can refer to Russia or Paris but not to fictional characters because they do not 'exist'. But I am arguing for a relationship which is consistent with the shifting, culturally relative, and often metaphorical frameworks through which we 'see' the world in the first place. For the interpretative critic, as opposed to the philosopher, is only motivated to point out text to world correspondences if he thinks that these are of pragmatic implicative significance. This would not of course be possible if texts did not in fact project worlds or situations with the same basic categorical structure that we use for the external world. But the common language for description in both will guarantee this, and it is in any case perfectly obvious to any reader that many texts do represent fairly fully articulated worlds, in which personal identity, causality, and so on, operate as they do in our own. That, after all, was the basis for the full-blown mimetic theory of art that we are now modifying.[8] We are modifying it by saying that any assertion of a text–world correspondence that goes beyond the recognition of factual adequacy, will depend on an interpreter's mediating statements. These statements (which we shall see are typical for all interpretations concerned with mimesis and its ideological consequences) will always obey the underlying logical form 'this (text/, co-text of situation) is like/unlike this (external world, context of situation) in X respects'. The respects are not in the text, but are contributed by the interpreter and can be more or less well founded. We will thus depend upon interpretative conventions for the 'vraisemblable' which obey cultural codes of only relative certainty. This is why I said that the simple mimetic theory needs modification. For as we shall see, these mediating codes take up inherently disputable ideological positions. Indeed the vraisemblable of the interpreter is always ideological, as I showed in attacking Riffaterre's view of history. The interpreter may thus treat the text as a hypothesis: he asks, is the text like the world in any significant respects? For no text alone, historical or fictional, can guarantee this relationship; we have to see and accept it. The interpreter's mediation is nevertheless part of our normal cognitive competence, and does not simply, or even particularly, apply to literary text. As Pratt points out, it is involved in the invention of 'scenarios' by strategists, hypothetical situations in philosophical argument, assumptions made 'for the sake of argument', speculations about 'what would he do next', and so on.[9]

In reminding ourselves of the hypothetical status of literary works we do not simply try to avoid useless discussion concerning the non-assertive or 'pseudo-statement' nature of literature, which tends to run counter to our intuition that writers seem to assert something and are to be taken seriously.[10] For there is also a positive side to the argument: literature, which is open to life, as is so often asserted, is in fact a particularly good source of assertions, judgements, and information. And by provoking comparison, it makes us question the nature of reality or of human character. We may ask whether the text is consonant with our knowledge, or whether it might extend it if we took seriously the notion that it might be true.

Thus, having read Wordsworth (or indeed Hardy), are we inclined to believe that natural phenomena are in form and function *like* religious buildings? There are, on this basis all sorts of relationships between the text and the world, from the relatively trivial (Betsey Trotwood is just like my Aunt Mabel) to the historically and ideologically significant (as when Goldmann argues that Racinian tragedy reveals the essential structure of the relationship of the *noblesse de la robe* to the Kings of France[11]).

We may of course prefer not to do this, and to make the focus of our attention the internal thematics of the text, drawing from it a plethora of meaning, which we suppose to be related to the structure of the language (the Saussurean 'langue') without going on to urge an ideological use for it, a position in the world for the text. There is ultimately no logically coherent or reasonable way of legislating in favour of one of these modes of interpretation to the permanent detriment of the other. What is at issue is the pragmatic ends which interpretation may serve, from the search for the 'semantically rich reading experience', to the use of the text to gain insight into history. In fact, almost all modes of interpretation inevitably move to and fro between the two.

This dialectic between the text's internal and external relations is shown in much of the work of Roland Barthes, particularly in *S/Z*. (This study of Balzac's 'Sarrasine' also shows that within a broadly structuralist perspective in which codes are discriminated, prose narrative is as susceptible to close analysis as poetry.[12])

Barthes's basic premisses concerning reference and language seem at the outset to be very similar to those of Riffaterre: 'dépeindre, c'est faire dévaler le tapis des codes, c'est référer, non d'un langage à un référent, mais d'un code à un autre code. Ainsi le réalisme . . . consiste, non à copier le réel, mais à copier une copie (peinte) du réel' (61).[13] This rather Platonic argument asserts that the real is always 'différé', 'remis plus loin'; we are caught within 'la circularité infinie des codes'.[14] This is a closed system whose value lies in its coherence, of the kind argued for by Barthes in his *Critical Essays*:

> In itself a language is not true or false; it is or it is not valid, i.e., constitutes a coherent system of signs. The rules of literary language do not concern the conformity of that language to reality (whatever the claims of the linguistic school) but only its submission to the system of signs the author has established (and we must of course give the word system a very strong sense here).[15]

I have already suggested a number of objections to any such exclusively self-referential theory of meaning. They turned in part upon the notion of cultural salience, and this is precisely where Barthes gets into difficulties.[16] For he has a referential or cultural code too, which is supposed to contain all the cultural background and collective wisdom of the text (its frames of belief). This code is activated when for example Balzac says that the Comte de Lanty was 'ennuyeux comme un banquier'[17] or when he describes the 'salon splendide' in which the party that opens the story takes place:

> Là fourmillaient, s'agitaient et papillonnaient les plus jolies femmes de Paris, les plus riches, les mieux titrées, éclatantes, pompeuses, éblouissantes de diamants, des fleurs sur la tête, sur le sein, dans les cheveux, semées sur les robes ou en guirlandes à leurs pieds. C'étaient de légers frémissements, des pas voluptueux qui faisaient rouler les dentelles, les blouses, la mousseline, autour de leurs flancs délicats . . . (32)[18]

The semic code for Barthes (the code which summarizes the defining semantic features of a passage) here connotes, unsurprisingly 'richesse'; but further 'allusivement, une atmosphère d'adultère est désignée; elle connote Paris comme lieu d'immoralité (les fortunes Parisiennes, comme celle des Lanty, sont immorales)' (32).[19] This interpretation makes explicit part of the 'referential code', which summarizes the cultural background of the text and involves a 'psychologie ethnique: Paris'. This 'psychologie ethnique' implied by the text, of course arises from a descriptive passage typical of literature, whose generalizations may not be exactly reliable (for not all bankers are boring) but which do reflect certain belief structures or prejudices on whose presence within the audience the author relies. And indeed Barthes is not finally content to leave such descriptions simply as part of the play of codes, for he wobbles over to the alternative position, in which he mediates between the text and the world, when he attacks such descriptions from a mimetic point of view, as reflecting an unreliable dominant bourgeois ideology. He is, in our earlier terms, urging a dissimilarity between text and world when he asserts that such cultural codes come from 'un corpus de savoir, d'un livre anonyme dont le meilleur modèle est sans doute le Manuel Scolaire' (211).[20] Barthes thus attacks Balzac as an exploiter of these cultural assumptions, since his text is part of a literary and ideological system in which literary descriptions, taken for truth, bolster up ideology. According to Barthes all such 'classic' texts imply their own Flaubertian 'Dictionary of Accepted Ideas'—indeed this is part of their definition as classic. Thus the codes

> quoique d'origine entièrement livresque, par un tourniquet propre à l'idéologie bourgeoise, qui inverse la culture en nature, semblent fonder le réel, la 'vie'. La 'vie' devient alors, dans le texte classique, un mélange écœurant d'opinions courantes, une nappe étouffante d'idées reçues : c'est en effet dans ces codes culturels que se concentre le démodé Balzacien, l'essence de ce qui, dans Balzac, ne peut être [ré-écrit.] (211)[21]

Barthes thus urges that the referential codes are a matter of literary convention ('entièrement livresque'), which we may falsely suppose to obtain in the culture which existed outside the text. They should thus be viewed with suspicion (as they were indeed by Flaubert in *Bouvard and Pécuchet*). Roger Fowler points out further and at length that the REF or referential code invokes not simply a 'corpus de savoir' but also a notion of point of view, of narrative authority.[22] The universe of values thus created is that of the narrator, in intimate relationship to an audience and not simply that of society at large: as may be, worldly, hedonistic, sceptical, ironic. Bourgeois (or any other) values thus interact within the rhetorical, generalizing stance of a narrator, who modifies the 'voix collective, anonyme, dont l'origine est la sapience humaine' ('the collective and anonymous voice whose origin is in human wisdom'). His voice relativizes the ideologies which the interpreter Barthes pretends are absolute.

Such uses of the text by the interpreter will be of central concern to our chapter on ideology, and so I do not wish to pursue the matter here, except to point out very briefly the possible positions for the reader/interpreter/text/external world relationship, which have been adumbrated so far. (Of course no critical theory could ever specify these relationships exhaustively, since they will depend ultimately on our varying states of knowledge and ignorance).

The first is that of recognition or assent: our state of knowledge is such that we already *know* whether the text is factually correct or incorrect (or probable or improbable in other respects). Of course we more often judge that the text is like or unlike what we take the world to be. The recognition or discovery of this relationship is not simply a matter of the 'meaning of the text' (though of course it depends on it) as of its significance and hence use to us.[23] Indeed such judgements depend upon a conjunction of the statements of the text *and* of our interpretative statements about it. And this type of judgement applies equally to the historical and fictional text.

However, all such assertions about the truth or falsity of texts should depend, in this conjunction, upon our accepting a relationship of the text to the world that is mediated not simply by interpretative assertion, but also by further evidence. We may well ask after reading Kafka, is the world truly anguish-ridden and absurd? But we cannot simply look further at the text; we have to find out, as a matter of fact, whether it is like the world in the relevant respects. It may be worth noting at this stage the curious fact that, as any reader of literary criticism will know, this citing of further evidence is rarely made except in an historical scholarship that is already beginning to look rather out of fashion. I have in mind examples like that of L. W. Tancock, who patiently points out that a reader of Zola's *Germinal* in 1885 might falsely suppose that it was an exact picture of the mining industry at that time. Its action supposedly takes place in 1867: but legislation had since removed the worst abuses, and the Russian anarchist missionary Souvarine really belongs to a much later period, of the various anarchist outrages of the late seventies and early eighties: 'The resulting composite picture of events at Montsou contains old abuses long since modified or put right and modern developments of socialism unknown in 1867. It is a grandiose epic of human misery and the revolt of the oppressed, but it is in no sense a true account of affairs as they could have existed at a given time.'[24] (Similar considerations have been urged concerning Dickens's treatment of the Poor Law in *Oliver Twist* and of Chancery in *Bleak House*.)

We more usually find the interpreter mediating the relationship between text and world on his own authority, depending on recognitional assent rather than on further evidence. The authority of the text devolves upon that of the interpreter. We can see how this happens in the case of Leavis's interpretation of D. H. Lawrence. In writing of *The Rainbow* he asserts 'the peculiar Lawrentian sense of the paradox of personal relations, especially of those between a man and a woman which make and validate a marriage; the insistence that, the more intimate and essential the relations, the more must the intimacy itself be, for the two lives that are brought into so essential a contact, a mutual acceptance of their separateness and otherness.'[25]

We have so far what might pass as a paraphrase of Lawrence, plus an implied moral recommendation. Leavis then goes on to make larger claims. We have 'the constatation' that 'Lawrence sees what the needs are, and understands their nature, so much better than George Eliot.'[26] Thus Ursula is superior to George Eliot's Maggie in *The Mill on the Floss* because of the 'more penetrating . . . insight (Lawrence) brings from life, from his experience and observation', which Leavis thereby himself implies to be correct.[27] Indeed Lawrence's scope for telling us the truth is according to Leavis, pretty well unlimited. He 'expresses in the latter part of the book (*The Rainbow*) the sense of the human problems as they were in contemporary civilisation which has its profound and complete expression in *Women in Love*'.[28]

One might well ask what independent evidence is or could be cited for so whole-hearted an endorsement of the writings of a novelist; or indeed for the real nature and dominance of bourgeois ideology for Barthes and Balzac, so as to license the view that 'Sarrasine' reflects it? Such critics rely upon their own authority and some form of recognitional assent on our part. This may be all very well, and reveals a great deal about the authority of the critic or interpreter in contemporary culture, but it remains a way of relating the text to the world that is not epistemologically very well founded. Such mediations are, as we have noted, peculiarly ideological, and we will have to look at this aspect of them more closely at a later stage. But I wish now to return to the second, less confident side of the dialectic I noted at the outset, and to a mode of interpretation which wishes to destroy all these apparent certainties by showing that the text, and hence our interpretation of it, may have a much less stable relationship to the world than we suppose. For we seem to have been driven to reassert that confident relationship of text to world implicit in our earlier trust in 'literal' language, here transposed to a trust in facts or evidence. Although this trust can never be shown to be wholly misplaced, since some common ground of agreement is necessary for intelligibility, we can by a generalization of some of Derrida's arguments concerning metaphor, be brought to see that this confidence presupposes a larger framework of belief. The consequences of holding to such a framework, and its inherent deficiencies, are matters of which we ought to be aware.

Post-structuralist 'deconstructive' criticism has worked hardest to bring such deficiencies sceptically to light; and we now come to an account of its methods for doing so.

5.1 Deconstruction and Scepticism

Nearly all the problems that deconstruction poses for criticism can be seen in outline in the work of Jacques Derrida. However, it should be said at the outset that the relatively firm positions which I (and others) will attribute to him in what follows, are in fact alien to his own method, which is 'slippery' and in a perpetual movement of self-qualification. My justification can only be that we thus see more clearly how Derrida can be 'used' (even if inevitably misinterpreted) in the common practice of literary interpretation. Derrida's critique was initially applied to philosophical texts in the main, but the difficulties (aporias or self-engendered paradoxes) he finds in them are found also in literature. According to him, philosophy can be seen as an infinitely extensible line of texts, all of which attempt to point out contradictions within their predecessors : but which will themselves be prone to internal contradiction. This is because they are themselves impossibly involved in a logocentric 'metaphysic of presence' as they perpetually and falsely imply or state (as literary texts can) their own satisfactory relationship to the external world.

This attack has two aspects which are worth distinguishing. Firstly Derrida believes, correctly, that most philosophers hitherto have proceeded on the assumption that they could fit language to the world : that there can be a satisfactory word–thing relationship. This confidence Derrida wishes to deny and supplant, by turning it upside down. We do not start with a 'reliable' language or an immediate relationship between word and thing ('presence') or indeed with knowledge at all. These are all things we aim at, and fail to attain. Philosophy expresses a perpetually deferred desire for mastery. This mode of attack (which is not essentially new) is now invading traditional Anglo-American philosophy. Thus Richard Rorty in *Philosophy and the Mirror of Nature* produces a number of arguments consistent with Derrida's which urge that any such search for epistemological certainty in philosophy is doomed to failure. All the foundations upon which we may wish to base it will let us down. There never can be a single over-all theory of anything, and hermeneutics, in looking critically at the language in which such arguments are framed, helps us to show this:

The notion that there is a permanent neutral framework whose 'structure' philosophy can display is the notion that the objects to be confronted by the mind, or the rules which sustain inquiry, are common to all discourse, or at least to every discourse upon a given topic. Thus epistemology proceeds on the assumption that all contributions to a given discourse are commensurable. Hermeneutics is largely a struggle against these assumptions.[1]

Derrida's second related line of attack is upon what he calls the 'transcendental signified' which may indeed be thought of as a kind of reality principle, 'un concept indépendant de la langue'[2], a mimetic check upon the possible meanings of any text. Thus we may in the past have appealed to the notions of God, man, telos, etc., or, as Leavis did, to the notions of the ideal marriage, or even to the notion of character itself. All this must be abolished, because to appeal to them is to cut off by an illegitimate interpretative summary that perpetual play of linguistic differences of which (says Derrida) all texts are constituted. This play ensures that 'aucun mot, aucun concept, aucun énoncé majeur ne viennent résumer et commander' ('no word, no concept, no greater statement can come along to summarize or command it').[3] Thus Hartman follows Derrida in saying that no author can be subjected to 'a dominant subject, whether identified as author, cogito, archetype or field of knowledge'.[4] The text is thus decentred and liberated for an indeterminate 'free play'.

If Derrida and those who think like him are right, there can never be any single coherent system of philosophy or *a fortiori* of interpretation (because the philosophical defence of any single system of interpretation will itself be metaphysically misconceived and prone to contradiction). And further, all texts which we are moved to try to situate satisfactorily in relationship to some external reality (to assert an origin, a presence, or as we have done a 'situation' for the text) are in fact perpetually undoing themselves in their evolution towards an unattainable goal.

Thus whatever we attempt in philosophy or interpretation, we proliferate structures no one of which, and no part of which, can be privileged over the others, either as 'original' or as offering a stopping-place. Each part of the text is linked explicitly or inexplicitly, to other parts of its (Saussurean) system, through which we are encouraged to travel, without much hope of arrival:

Que ce soit dans l'ordre du discours parlé ou du discours écrit, aucun élément ne peut fonctionner comme signe sans renvoyer à un autre élément qui lui-même n'est pas simplement présent. Cet enchaînement fait que chaque 'élément', phonème ou graphème, se constitue à partir de la trace en lui des autres éléments de la chaine ou du système.[5]

We are caught in a systematic play of difference which we can only it seems arrest in bad faith,[6] and which we will never be able to master.

For Derrida and others seem to assert, so far as interpretation is concerned, that if all meaning is part of a system, the pursuit of any one meaning would then involve unravelling or following through the whole system. (Compare the fantasy of looking up a word in a dictionary and travelling the whole way through it.) Thus the 'full' meaning of any word, phrase or text will never simply stop and declare itself, for there will always be a further nuance to pursue, and according to Derrida's critical practice—and that of Hartman when he most closely follows him, in *Saving the Text*—there will always be a further 'différance', by which neologism Derrida means both the discrimination and destruction of contrasted differences, and the consequent deferring—or 'délai, délégation, renvoi, détour, retard, mise en réserve' ('delay, delegation, sending back, detour, holding up, or putting in reserve')[7]—of any coming at the full meaning of the signifier's signified. Derrida puts the matter this way, in conjunction with his anti-mimetic thesis, that language always pretends or aims to make things present to us, but always fails to do so:

> When we cannot take hold of or show the thing, let us say the present, the being present, when the present does not present itself, then we signify, we go through the detour of signs . . . The sign would thus be a deferred presence . . . Now this classical determination presupposes that the sign is conceivable only on the basis of the presence that it defers and in view of the deferred presence that one intends to reappropriate . . . [But] the signified concept is never present in itself, in an adequate presence that would refer only to itself. Every concept is necessarily and essentially inscribed in a chain or system, within which it refers to another and to other concepts, by the systematic play of differences, such a play then—difference—is no longer simply a concept but the possibility of conceptuality.[8]

Derrida's assertions concerning the (deferred) nature of meaning would have two main effects on interpretation. The first is sceptical : if there is no stopping-place we literally never arrive at a certain interpretation. The second is subjective : if we thus refuse to stop, what are the 'rules' for the play of meaning thus discerned? Do they simply depend upon the whim and ingenuity of the interpreter? And further, do these two consequences, taken together, imply that interpretation itself must be involved in a perpetual and solipsistic regress, as our playful determinations of the play of the text are themselves seen to be subject to a Derridan critique?

For Derrida's position is, as he himself acknowledges, subject to its own basic aporia or contradiction : to have force it has to presuppose that very premiss of objectivity (for the literary text, of an external mimetic standpoint) that it is out to destroy: 'nous ne pouvons énoncer aucune proposition déstructrice qui n'ait déjà du se glisser dans la forme, dans la logique et les postulations implicites de cela meme qu'elle voulait contester. Pour prendre un exemple parmi tant d'autres: c'est à l'aide du concept de *signe* qu'on ébranle la métaphysique de la présence.'[9] The sign seems not only to be a constant and 'privileged' object, but also to be a sign *of* something (a 'signifié'). Not only are deconstructive arguments contaminated by the system they have to stay inside in order to criticize, but they presuppose objectivity in all their references to that system, particularly summary ones— 'Rousseau says that . . .' and so on. (Derrida is almost puritanically accurate in his reference to texts which he also in some sense privileges, or makes into 'transcendental signifieds'.) Derrida is of course aware of this type of objection, which makes his 'grammatology' an essentially strategic interpretative exercise: 'La grammatologie serait sans doute moins une autre science, une nouvelle discipline chargée d'un nouveau contenu, d'un nouveau domaine bien déterminé, que la pratique vigilante de ce partage textuel'.[10]

This 'textual division' involves a strategy of deconstructive reading, in which we see that the arguments of the text put into question their own premisses and their own consistency. Thus although Saussure sees spoken language as primary and writing as derivative, he suppresses, according to Derrida, the notion of language as (essentially) a written signifying system, which goes beyond and in fact surrounds any individual act of speech.[11] This suppression leads Saussure into contradiction because of his failure to see that writing is in fact the precondition of language. (This is of course one of those peculiarly transcendental philosopher's arguments about logical priority rather than genetic ordering.) Ultimately perhaps this question of priority cannot be decided : what Derrida is trying to show, I think, is that any attempt to come down on one side or the other disregards the dialectical interdependence of the two modes of expression, which deserves examination. It is with such arguments that Derrida can, when he comes to discuss Rousseau, show that his (written) argument in favour of speech as the 'natural' condition of language, of speech as so to speak politically untrammelled, uncorrupted by culture, in fact itself, as made in writing, confirms the priority of writing, and reveals the merely mythical status of any argument for an 'origin' of language in a speech which is merely 'supplemented' by writing.[12] Indeed speech is always part of the system of text, since it always implies that system of language (of 'difference') which the text typically encodes.

If Derrida's arguments are construed, as they usually have been[13] as *inter alia* an attack on the stability of the arguments within a literary text as urged in conventional criticism, then this attack can only be made from what seems to be a sceptical view of the relationship between speech and writing or language and the world, which itself claims a superior certainty. This remains true, particularly in literary interpretation, in which an apparently transparent or 'reliable' relationship between text and world is attacked because the text can be shown to display all the signs of fictivity or literary convention, or metaphor. For as we saw in reporting Derrida's 'White Mythology' in Chapter 2, the apparently logical distinctions upon which all texts depend may 'really' be part of a proliferating and potentially misleading series of metaphorical frameworks which are both unreliable by the exalted standards of philosophy, and yet inescapable. We are thus caught, as interpreters concerned for truth, in a perpetual dialectic between logic and rhetoric.

Given then that if we follow Derrida we know that we are implicated within the systems we attack, indeed forced to presuppose them, we can see that deconstruction is an opportunistic method, one of strategic dislocation, a criticism from within. As Derrida puts it:

notre discours appartient irréductiblement au système des oppositions métaphysiques. On ne peut annoncer la rupture de cette appartenance que par une *certaine* organisation, un certain aménagement *stratégique* qui, à l'intérieur du champ et de ses pouvoirs propres, retournant contre lui ses propres *stratagèmes*, produise une *force de dislocation* se propageant à travers tout le système, le fissurant dans tous les sens et le *dé-limitant* de part en part.[14]

If this is the case then we have to consider those points at which deconstruction is pragmatically most effective, and thus to consider the ideological ends which it might be thought to serve. It is this strategic sense, the feel for the weak points in our unquestioned thinking, that constitutes Derrida's strength. The points I have made in this brief introduction will have to be exemplified in what follows, but they do allow us to say that Derridan deconstruction will present us with at least four main problems. These are, firstly, the attempted abolition of anything in the world external to the text or anything privileged within it, that will help us to determine its meaning (an anti-mimetic, free-play thesis). Secondly, the attack, or apparent attack, on the text as condemned to incompleteness, and to self-contradiction because of its own unforeseen implications. This is because reading and interpretation must always aim at a certain relationship, unperceived by the writer, between what he commands and what he does not command of the patterns of language he uses. Thirdly, the problem of establishing under these circumstances criteria for interpretation of the text which do not simply reflect the ingenuity of the critic as he plays about in intertextual space, and so can meet the charge of irrelevant subjectivism. For fourthly, if Derrida is right, all interpretation which respects the nature of language is condemned to indeterminacy.

5.2 Ambiguity and Self-contradiction

When we call a book realistic, we mean that it is relatively free from bookish artificialities; it convinces us, where more conventional books do not. It offers us *realiora*, if not *realia*, as Eugene Zamyatin succinctly puts it; not quite the real things, but things that seem more real than those offered by others. By rereading these other books too and reconstructing their conventions, we can relate them to our comparatively realistic book and specify its new departures more precisely. We can define realism by its context.[1]

The deconstructionist view of the literary text as inherently self-contradictory really depends upon a play of this kind between our construction of a context of situation and literary convention. To put the matter crudely, the assumption is that the reader expects nothing but a transparent version of the former, and is thus undeceived when he is persuaded by the critic that the text depends upon the latter. Literary language thus gestures toward an end which is perpetually subverted : for the very conventions by which the gesture is made (towards 'reality' or 'truth' or the 'transcendental signified') will reveal fictional (i.e. unsatisfactory representational, or non-referential) conventions. Where we expect the literal we find the metaphorical; where we expect realism we find literary convention, where we expect something to be made present to us, we find that it is perpetually put off or deferred.

Under this sort of examination the text is perpetually ironized. It is shown to be ambiguous, not so much by way of praise, as in New Critical method, designed to reveal a 'richness of meaning' which is ultimately reconciled through irony, paradox, and so on, but at its own expense. For the author often seems unaware of his inability to achieve his aims. Indeed once the notion of a free play of language is allowed to take over, the author, as director of our attention to aspects of reality, and for much else, can be dispensed with.[2]

Thus the writer's attempt to reveal the world to us by taking a particular view of it, by thematizing it, or by projecting a situation which may be construed as like what we know of the world, may always be compromised by the language he uses:

Though X's works are always suggesting the possibility of some ultimate reference point for making sense of the world, they no sooner do so than they defer the presentation of this reference point or expose its purely fictive or purely arbitrary nature. X's works dramatise or put into play a variety of ways of ordering reality, all of which are seen finally, as already *written* and therefore without privileged authority. Ultimately, X's works are commentaries on their own inability to transcend the interpretive function they proffer, and this problem of interpretation is passed on to the reader. What these works are really about then is their unreadability, which is to say the reader's struggle to impose his own preferred fictions upon them.[3]

It is not difficult to generate readings on this basis : for if all texts which display various kinds of fictional conventions are to be seen as implicitly about those conventions, and if the conventions are not allowed to be self-consciously or critically used by the author (as they are in the experimental self-deconstructing text, for example) then the text, and the author's implicit aim, once put into contradiction, are prone to deconstruction. Gerald Graff, whom I cited above, attacks an interpretation by Hillis Miller for obeying this type of prescription.[4] For the central assumption that Miller and critics like him make is that the writer's method, and his metaphors in particular, 'never point to reality but draw us back into their own infinite problematics'.[5] Miller cites Dickens's *Sketches by Boz*, which seem to have been attempting a straightforward mimetic realism based on London in 1836. But this is an illusion held by writer and reader, because Boz as narrator 'must tell lies, employ fictions, in ways which expose the fact that they are lies'.[6] The text calls its own status into question through its use of theatrical metaphors, its references to other literary works, and its references to the imagination's tendency to impose its own 'romantic humour' on what it describes. This conveys to the deconstructive critic the moral that 'social reality, far from being solid and determinate, is itself a kind of "text" that persistently eludes interpretation.'[7] Thus alerted we can see that the text uses 'highly artificial schemas inherited from the past' which lead to the imposition of 'fictitious patterns' on reality.[8] Graff comments rather sourly on this claim that Miller does not seem to consider that such patterns might on the contrary themselves bear some determinable relation to historical circumstances; and with our arguments concerning cultural salience and the interpreter's mediation on the grounds of likeness in mind, we might sympathize with him. Miller can only be pretending to be taken in for the sake of a very shaky sceptical argument.[9]

The aim of such interpretation is thus to display the 'problematics' of literary language in such a way as to cast doubt upon the claim of the literary text to give us knowledge or direct us to the world, and thus further to prevent the critic from attempting to mediate between the one and the other. The argument is in fact the opposite of that we first presented concerning metaphor, and a sceptical extrapolation of the second which we drew from Derrida. But we have argued that the text *can* be seen to be relevant to its historical context—from Chamfort's remark, through Yeats's adaptation of Plato, to 'Yew Trees' and Balzac's vision of Paris.

Deconstructive analysis can therefore only work successfully in two ways: (1) by persuading us of the 'fictionality' of all discourse and hence of the *provisionality* of all the mediations I have argued for: and (2), more strategically, in finding particular problematic texts of which its assertions can be seen to be true. The first line of argument can be resisted only to the extent that we resisted Lakoff and Johnson : the second is most successful when it finds texts which seem to play with, or set up in dialectical contradiction or competition, different modes of organizing reality, i.e. those whose pragmatic grounds of acceptance are not well assured. (It is thus not surprising that texts by Artaud, Freud, Lacan, and Mallarmé seem prone to Derrida's approach.) One could say for example that much of the work of Wallace Stevens has always been sceptically deconstructive, since it so obviously doubts the adequacy of language to reality, and indulges in a play with metaphor, as in 'An Ordinary Evening in New Haven' and many other poems.

These sceptical consequences of deconstruction are strongly urged by de Man in a much cited article analysing a passage of Proust which seems to him to dramatize two possible ways of organizing experience, one of many in which 'Proust dramatizes tropes by means of landscapes or descriptions of objects'.[10] The passage turns for de Man on the distinction between the metaphorical and the metonymic, where the metaphor depends on (paradigmatic) similarity in much the sense we have described, and the metonymic mode may be thought of as a syntagmatic, contiguous one, the patient adding of observation to observation, of contingent fact to fact.[11] The analysis depends upon an exploitation of our doubts concerning the boundaries of the literal and the metaphorical. In discussing Proust, de Man tries to correlate these two features with what he calls 'grammar' (i.e. the tendency to universality of meaning and univocality of language, or adequacy to reality) and rhetoric (the peculiarly literary use of trope and figuration, which may subvert the logic of 'grammar'). In showing how these concepts apply to the text, he leads us into paradox. The passage he cites is the following one:

I had stretched out on my bed, with a book, in my room which sheltered, tremblingly, its transparent and fragile coolness against the afternoon sun, behind the almost closed blinds through which a glimmer of daylight had nevertheless managed to push its yellow wings, remaining motionless between the wood and the glass, in a corner, poised like a butterfly. It was hardly light enough to read, and the sensation of the light's splendour was given me only by the noise of Camus . . . hammering dusty crates; resounding in the sonorous atmosphere that is peculiar to hot weather, they seemed to spark off scarlet stars; and also by the flies executing their little concert, the chamber music of summer: evocative not in the manner of a human tune that, heard perchance during the summer, afterwards reminds you of it ; it is connected to summer by a more necessary link : born from beautiful days, resurrecting only when they return, containing some of their essence, it does not only awaken their image in our memory; it guarantees their return, their actual, persistent, unmediated presence.

The dark coolness of my room related to the full sunlight of the street as the shadow relates to the ray of light, that is to say it was just as luminous and it gave my imagination the total spectacle of the summer, whereas my senses, if I had been on a walk, could only have enjoyed it by fragments; it matched my repose which (thanks to the adventures told by my book and stirring my tranquillity) supported, like the quiet of a motionless hand in the middle of a running brook, the shock and the motion of a current of activity.[12]

Although de Man's prose is peculiarly opaque, and the distinctions he wishes to make often irritatingly unclear because of his variations on normal usage (for example that between grammar and rhetoric[13]), I think his argument is as follows. The passage turns on the difference between the actual inspection (by 'fragments') of the world outside the room for the 'real' aspects of summer in 'experience', i.e. metonymically; and the assertion that the taking of those elements of it which penetrate the room imagistically, as symbolic, evocative of summer ('the sensations of sunlight's splendour' etc.) will suffice for the narrator as a kind of metaphor of summer. 'The dark coolness of my room . . . gave my imagination the total spectacle of the summer, whereas my senses, if I had been on a walk, could only have enjoyed it by fragments.' Metaphorical likeness is thus supposed to triumph over fragmentary fact, for metonymy is random and contingent, whereas metaphor depends on the 'necessary link' which leads to 'perfect synthesis' (134). Thus Marcel brings the passage to a climax with a simile: 'the dark coolness of my room . . . supported, like the quiet of a motionless hand in the middle of a running brook, the shock and motion of a torrent of activity.'

Now de Man, if I interpret him correctly, sees this as paradoxical, just as I would do, because the metaphorical component in this antithesis will itself analyse out into metonymical parts : as de Man attempts to show when he looks at the metaphor of the brook (which he rather unconvincingly 'deconstructs' to show its use of a hidden metonymy), because the phrase 'torrent of activity' depends on a cliché whose coupling of words is governed 'not by the necessary link that reveals their potential identity, but by the contingent habit of proximity' (135–6). Metaphor and simile convey no necessary insights. The concluding simile thus connotes, according to de Man, coolness in metaphorical relation to the room, and heat in metonymic cliché-ridden relation to the world of activity outside the room. This metonymic reliance undermines what is seen as Proust's assertion of the superiority of metaphor in this passage, and so 'the deconstructive reading reveals a first paradox: the passage valorises metaphor as being the "right" literary figure, but then proceeds to constitute itself by an epistemologically incompatible figure of metonymy' (139–40). This is a very complicated and in the end I think unconvincing argument, particularly if my view is correct, that the metonymic implications of metaphor, far from being epistemo-logically 'incompatible' with it, are simply the interpretation by which it becomes intelligible to the reader. De Man's argument nevertheless reveals a typical deconstructive strategy at the level of language, as he himself is at pains to assert: 'after the deconstructive reading of the Proust passage we can no longer believe in the assertion made in this passage about the intrinsic, metaphysical superiority of metaphor over metonymy. We seem to end up in a mode of negative assurance that is highly productive of critical discourse' (137).

Now this really amounts to saying that whatever writers may claim, they can't give us 'metaphysical' insights into reality.[14] It is at base an attack on intuition as manifested in metaphor (or more typically symbol) as being insight without evidence—a claim made by many Symbolist writers.[15] But we have shown in our analysis of metaphor that such evidence may be forthcoming even in the case of metaphor, if we are satisfied in our search for the grounds of its likeness in the external world. These grounds are of course not 'necessary', but they are such as one might rationally accept. However, de Man does not trust the text to arouse such discriminat-ory mediating powers in the reader. For he goes on to assert that 'the whole of literature' would give way to this type of epistemological attack, in which 'criticism is the deconstruction of literature, the reduction to rigours of grammar of rhetorical mystifications. And if we hold up Nietzsche as the philosopher of such a critical deconstruction, then the literary critic would become the philo-sopher's ally in his struggle with the poets' (138).

The good point that de Man is making is that deconstruction puts literature and philosophy on the same footing. It discusses rhetoric within philosophy and philosophical claims within the rhetoric of fictions. This is why so much of Derrida's work looks like literary criticism and so much of de Man's like philosophy.[16] The literary and the philosophical (or psychological, or any) text are subject to the same type of analysis. Thus de Man asserts that 'literature turns out to be the main topic of philosophy and the kind of truth to which it aspires.'[17] It is the competition or struggle between them that turns out to be de Man's main concern: his critical insight is supposed to rise above literature's blindness. Again and again he deprives writers of the goals for which they appear to be striving.[18] For example, 'The meanings [of Rousseau's texts] can be said to be ethical, religious, or eudaimonic, but each of these thematic categories is torn apart by the aporia that constitutes it, thus making the categories effective to the precise extent that they eliminate the value system in which their classification is grounded.'[19] Thus Rousseau when he 'confesses' to his guilt is supposed to be 'sincere' and yet at the same time excuses himself when he gives his actions a narrative context. His rhetorical strategy explains his actions in a way that dissolves responsibility.

This is made clear in de Man's analysis of the famous incident in the *Confessions* in which Rousseau, while employed as a servant in an aristocratic Turin household, steals a pink and silver coloured ribbon, and when the theft is discovered, accuses a young maidservant of having given it to him, thus implying that she was trying to seduce him. Rousseau is of course attempting to be as frank as possible, and is well aware that he may excuse himself 'by means of what conforms to the truth'.[20] But this for de Man is not enough; he has in any case other sins of which to convict him:

Qui s'accuse s'excuse; this sounds convincing and convenient enough, but, in terms of absolute truth, it ruins the seriousness of any confessional discourse by making it self-destructive. Since confession is not a reparation in the realm of practical justice but exists only as a verbal utterance, how then are we to know that we are indeed dealing with a *true* confession, since the recognition of guilt implies its exoneration in the name of the same transcendental principle of truth that allowed for the certitude of guilt in the first place?[21]

He is concerned that the theft turns on a matter of (verifiable) fact, whereas a confession turns on a mere verbal performance which reveals a sincere feeling only if we take the performer's word for it. An excuse, and the claim to feel shame, are thus peculiarly unverifiable. This is, I think, so, to the degree that one cannot test the sincerity of a text, in the way that one may be able to test the sincerity of a person by interrogation. (Though de Man thinks he can also do this, as we shall see.) The argument is that true confession and excuse within a narrative are somehow logically incompatible, and that a text which attempts to reconcile the two will *ipso facto* deconstruct itself. For the transgressor will never be able to prove the sincerity of his guilt in the way that he can prove the facts of his crime. It does not seem to occur to de Man that if he is right this is generally true, both inside and outside literature. It should nevertheless be noted that he feels that with the help of Freud he can get round the question of sincerity as well. He thus does not simply tie up the text in a confusion between confession and excuse, but also convicts Rousseau of a subconscious purpose which would in any case destroy any attempt at moral sincerity. Subconscious self-deceit combines with rhetorical self-contradiction: thus de Man combines epistemological doubt with a great deal of moral certainty, in accusing Rousseau of sins which it would be difficult to verify by his own standards.

One is more ashamed of the exposure of the desire to expose oneself than of the desire to possess; like Freud's dreams of nakedness, shame is primarily exhibitionistic. What Rousseau *really* wanted is neither the ribbon nor Marion, but the public scene of exposure which he actually gets . . . This desire is truly shameful, for it suggests that Marion was destroyed, not for the sake of Rousseau's saving face, nor for the sake of his desire for her, but merely in order to provide him with a stage on which to parade his disgrace, or, what amounts to the same thing, to furnish him with a good ending for Book II of his *Confessions*. (285)

De Man seems to believe that all texts will be prone to this type of deconstruction, that 'a literary text simultaneously asserts and denies the authority of its own rhetorical mode', so that 'poetic writing' is in itself 'the most advanced and refined mode of deconstruction'.[22] However, this assertion concerning poetic writing is either made true by definition or obviously over-generalized. I think that we can only grasp the true force of deconstruction if we apply it to texts which, like the multiply ambiguous poetic text, may exploit our tendency to give it contradictory readings by playing with the difference of meaning within language. Mallarmé's explicit syntactic and homonymic ambiguities are so complex that no 'single' reading of his poems can be given, as almost any commentary on his work may show.[23] Many of his lines offer a choice of readings based not alone on the ambiguity of descriptive terms, but upon the syntax of the sentence. As the choices thus generated proliferate through his poems, the possible number of ways through them multiply. The 'deconstructive' element enters when we realize that the result is a large number of incompatible affirmations, so that the notion of assertion itself becomes problematic.

However the play of difference in the ambiguous syntax and semantics of Mallarmé, although it may appear to extend our notions of ambiguity, place the burden of choice on the reader (who cannot look for a single 'true' interpretation), and show how language may be self-referentially problematic, does not yet have that strategic or ideological importance that we said was often the motive for effective deconstruction. What we need is a mode of Derridan analysis that leads to a more painful doubt concerning the adequacy and interrelation of the conceptual frameworks we impose on the text in interpreting it. (I am not sure that de Man on excuses meets this criterion. He basically points to the logic of some essentially unverifiable first person avowals; which is a commonplace of moral philosophy.)

Just such a strategically effective interpretation is brilliantly provided by Barbara Johnson on Melville's 'Billy Budd'. She uses the Derridan notion of 'difference' to show that within the text, 'the difference between entities (prose and poetry, men and women, literature and theory, guilt and innocence) are shown to be based on a repression of differences *within* entities, ways in which an entity differs from itself.'[24] That is, the interpreter of the text cannot depend upon crude oppositions, but must become aware of the way in which the distinctions to be made on either side of them may undermine our confidence in the opposition itself. Thus deconstruction attempts 'to follow the subtle, powerful effects of difference already at work within the illusion of a binary opposition' (xi). We tease out 'warring forces of significance within the text itself' (5) so that where we had expected to find unity we may find division. Thus the castrato Zambinella confuses Sarrasine's (and our) notions of sexual identity, and threatens our own through the theme of castration (10 f., 13 ff.). Where we thought we could interpret the text along the line of opposition (as many early structuralists did, inspired in part by Lévi-Strauss) we find that we cannot, because the text is more disturbingly subtle than that. The force of this lies in the interpreter's finding distinctions which actually cause bother and pain, such as those concerning justice as they arise in a reading of Melville's 'Billy Budd'.

For justice is and is not done to Billy, as the contradictory accounts of him (the trial report and the ballad after his death) suggest. The authority of these accounts (and of Captain Vere) is called into question. Billy is an innocent killer; Claggart is a perverted lying victim. Thus 'readers tend either to save the plot and

condemn Billy ('acceptance', 'tragedy', or 'necessity') or to save
Billy and condemn the plot ('irony', 'justice', or 'social criticism')
(2), so that Billy's 'God bless Captain Vere' can be interpreted in
both ways. It is Johnson's purpose to deconstruct this simple
opposition, and she does so in a detail which defies summary. What
is put into question is the relation between a man's nature and his
acts, between Billy's denial of plot, and his ensnarement within one,
between Billy the innocent literal reader and Claggart the dupli-
citous ironic reader (of one another's characters, one assumes,
though Johnson allegorizes the text at this point (83 ff.)). So that
'What the reader of 'Billy Budd' must do is to analyse what is at
stake in the very opposition between literality and irony' (85). A
psychoanalytic reading will similarly reveal contradictory perspectives within Billy and Claggart (89 f.), thus deconstructing any
simple opposition between them (for instance when we consider the
possible hidden motivation for Billy's spilling of the soup across
Claggart's path). Thus 'far from recounting an unequivocal clash of
opposites the confrontation between Billy and Claggart is built by a
series of minute gradations and subtle insinuations. The opposites
that clash here are not two *characters* but two *readings*' (97). Indeed
the most controversial character in the story is Captain Vere, whom
most interpreters have seen as the character who brings complexity
and ambiguity to the tale, as he comes to his decision and gives
reasons for it. For he cannot be so much concerned with moral traits,
as with the consequences of actions within a particular historical
situation. And for this he has a socially determined consensus to
judge by : those of the duties of a 'commissioned fighter'. Martial
law operates through him (100). (*Measure for Measure* can be seen
also to be concerned with the same sorts of irreconcilable moral
conflicts.) Absolute moral law and its associated 'reading' has, it
seems, to give way to the notion of an historical context. Our reading
of events is 'contextually mutable' : and yet Vere may be misusing
these justifications (the background of mutiny) so that we judge him
(100). History here, in Auden's words, may explain but it cannot
excuse or pardon.
As Melville himself writes:

In a *legal view* the apparent victim of the tragedy was he who has sought to
victimise a man blameless; and the indisputable deed of the latter, *morally
regarded*, so constituted the most heinous of military crimes. Yet more. The
essential right and wrong involved in the matter, the clearer that might be, so
much the worse for the responsibility of loyal sea commander, in as much as
he was not authorised to determine the matter on that primitive basis.[25]

Yet as Johnson points out 'it is precisely the determination of the proper frame of reference that dictates the outcome of the decision' (103). The Bible confronts the Mutiny Act. It forces a 'binary difference', between justice to character and political prudence where none should exist. Johnson seems to suggest at this point that all insoluble differences of this kind are the result of violence and power. We are not allowed to make a 'reading beyond politics' (107) and so Billy's act gives him up to the political judgement which Vere cannot avoid, even when aware of its moral injustice. Such oppositions are inherently deadly. Johnson can moralize her own reading : an awareness of Derridan difference and incompatibility may save the reader from an over-simplifying interpretation : but it cannot save Billy or Vere. The law court provides us with a little allegory of the relativity of interpretations, and a reminder of their pragmatic force as they lead to forgiveness or punishment.

So far as deconstruction is concerned then, it is the nature and indeed the co-textual situation of the particular text that licenses this mode of interpretation, since there surely are many texts which are immune from deconstructive scepticism of this kind. This may be because the present order of society and its associated conventions for interpretation are merely content to leave them so. But if this is accepted, we can appreciate the perhaps hardly coincidental fact that it is the contemporary experimental text, as practised by the French *nouveaux romanciers*, by Americans like Robert Coover, Ray Federman, Donald Barthelme, and Walter Abish, that deliberately embrace contradiction and aporia—usually those of literary convention itself. By deliberate self-contradiction and ambiguity they avoid any consistent mimetic commitment and thus allow the reader to play amongst the deliberately revealed techniques of the creative writer—John Barth's 'funhouse' of fiction in which one may as well be 'lost' as in Robbe-Grillet's labyrinth. The text deconstructs itself by involving the reader in incompatible strategies of comprehension.

This parallel between the arguments of the critic and the practice of the writer is seen most perspicuously in the case of Robbe-Grillet, who attacks the (logocentric) conventions of realism by attacking that art which provides for the reader 'l'idée toute faite qu'ils ont de la réalité', and turns the interest of his work around to his own inherently unreliable creative processes : 'L'invention, l'imagination deviennent à la limite le sujet du livre'.[26] In his work, and that of many others, the notion of 'presence' is banished by deliberate self-contradiction, so that the text is 'impossibly' ambiguous, and has to be seen as a form of play with language, with previous literary convention, and with its own 'thèmes générateurs': 'l'anecdote se met ainsi à foisonner: discontinue, plurielle, mobile, aléatoire, désignant elle-même sa propre fictivité, elle devient un "jeu" au sens plus fort du terme'.[27]

I have here presented the sceptical side of the deconstructive point of view. It attempts to reveal the unwilling (Dickensian) or willing (modern experimental) entrapment of the literary text in the aporias and contradictions of its own conventions. The corollary of this is the perpetual reminder by the interpreter of the provisional and fictive and unresolved nature of the text. And in the profoundest type of deconstruction this unresolved nature is one which it may have to share with the conceptual schema and philosophical beliefs upon which it depends. But I wish now to turn to the more positive side of the argument (paralleled by Robbe-Grillet's games) and to the way in which the text, once it is released from the logocentric assertion of presence or mimetic adequacy, may give rise to a free play of interpretative strategies.

5.3 Free Play

There are thus two interpretations of interpretation, of structure, of sign, of free play. The one seeks to decipher, dreams of deciphering, a truth or an origin which is free from free play or the order of the sign, and lives like an exile the necessity of interpretation. The other which is no longer turned towards the origin, affirms free play and tries to pass beyond man and humanism, the name of man being the name of that being who, throughout the history of metaphysics or ontotheology—in other words, throughout the history of all his history—has dreamed of full presence, the reassuring foundation, the origin and end of the game.[1]

Derrida's prescription here goes beyond those epistemologically attacking interpretations of the text which we have just looked at, where the search for self-contradiction seems to be performed in the light of a superior epistemological awareness—the insight of the interpreter revealing the blindness of the author, or the relativity or self-reference or self-contradiction of the frameworks he uses.

The release of the text into free play is different from this, but the basic assumptions of the interpretative method are the same. For once the text has been allowed a freedom from mimetic or situational commitment, then a Saussurean view of language allows us, using the text as a starting-point, to exercise considerable ingenuity in following its pathways.

Derrida's work in this field parallels that of Barthes, who emphasizes the value of this kind of critical activity or 'work': 'l'enjeu du travail littéraire, c'est de faire du lecteur, non plus un consommateur, mais un producteur du texte.'[2] We must give up our former certainties about meaning and the thematics of the text which made our attitude that of the consumer who, in accepting art as a mirror of reality, asks for more of what he knows or finds to his taste, and subjects it (or thematizes it) according to his own preferred 'transcendental signifieds'. We must engage in something more rigorous, not submitting ourselves to the text in declaring its conventional meaning, but in realizing its exploratory possibilities, which are potentially endless: 'interpréter un texte, ce n'est pas lui donner un sens (plus ou moins fondé, plus ou moins libre) c'est au contraire apprécier de quel pluriel il est fait . . . dans le texte idéal, les réseaux sont multiples et jouent entre eux . . . une galaxie de signifiants'.[3]

These systems interact in language 'comme un jeu' and the

'writerly' text thus conceived offers no centre or obvious opening for interpretation; it has no beginning, it is 'reversible', it has several entrances none of which is the main one.[4] The argument runs in parallel to that for experimental work, and the consequences for interpretation are clear: 'suivre cette entrée c'est viser au loin, non une structure légale de normes et d'écarts, une loi narrative ou poétique, mais une perspective (de bribes, de voix venues d'autres textes, d'autres codes) dont cependant le point de fuite est sans cesse reporté, mystérieusement ouvert.'[5] The interpreter in realizing this play of codes has also to realize something about himself. His thought-processes are to be no more simply determinable than those of the text: 'ce "moi" qui s'approche du texte est déjà lui-même une pluralité d'autres textes, de codes infinis . . . ou perdus.'[6] This looks like an invitation to a subjectivity which admits no restraints as it works a text which itself cannot be tied down in any way : 'La lecture ne consiste pas à arrêter la chaine des systèmes, à fonder une vérité.'[7]

Most modern critics, particularly since Empsonian new criticism, have tried to reveal a multiplicity of meaning in texts, and have indeed accepted the intertextual relationships implied in central modernist works like *Ulysses* or the *Cantos* or *The Waste Land*, where the voices may come from other texts, other codes. But the demonstrations were subordinated to specifiable ends—the psychological value of certain types of irony, or ambiguity as a valuable complexity in thought directed to particular themes or topics (as for example in Eliot on the Metaphysicals or Marvell), or to the hidden thematic *unification* of the multiply allusive text. All of this would be attacked by deconstructivists as privileging certain meanings and as all too premature. Such attempts to motivate a text by appeal to intention or psychological ends, or ideological attempts to impose thematic control over multiple meanings, would seem, if Derrida is to be believed, to have been abolished by the progress of his own style of interpretation: 'nous sommes donc d'entrée de jeu dans la devenir-immotivé du symbole . . . l'immotivation de la trace doit être maintenant entendue comme une opération et non comme un état, comme un mouvement actif, une dé-motivation, non comme une structure donnée.'[8]

What then does such a playful interpretation look like? We find that not only are the most peculiarly uncontrolled possibilities discerned for the text, but that the interpretation, as well as dismantling the text, will as often pause also to criticize and dismantle itself, as it perpetually reminds itself to draw away from the brink of objectivity, or the privileging of meaning. Each phase of the text, and of the interpretation, is deconstructed in turn. The process is thus a very self-conscious one. The text is read for its theory-generating nuances, and the theory of the practice of interpretation in the light of such nuances is also put at issue: 'Hence it generates a critical text very close to and yet very different from the ones it comments on: witness, in "The Supplement of Copula", the text of Derrida's deconstruction of Benveniste's deconstruction of Aristotle (via a partial deconstruction of Kant, Trendelenburg, Brunschvig, Cassirer, and Heidegger, all of whom had themselves partially deconstructed Aristotle)'.[9]

Much of the work of Derrida shows this process, but I have chosen to concentrate on a 'single' text, his 'Living On: Border Lines' which purports to be an interpretation of two literary texts by Maurice Blanchot, but is also an interpretation of itself. For Derrida provides us with two texts: a main discourse and a subtext below the line which comments on it, and thus threatens a perpetual regress. The first six pages are spent in mediation on its title and the two questions which follow it:

Living on

But who's talking about living?
In other words on living?
This time, 'in other words' does not put the same thing into other words, does not clarify an ambiguous expression, does not function like an 'i.e.'. It masses the power of indecision and adds to the foregoing utterance its capacity for skidding.[10]

As this marvellously rhetorical opening shows, things can perpetu- ally, as Derrida has argued, be put in 'other' words through the detours of language, and mighty indeed are the powers of indecision encountered along its multiplying paths, let alone the indetermin- able and unforeseen chances of skidding on them as we go along. For 'commentary' can only provide a 'textual supplement that calls in turn for an overdetermining "in other words" and so on and so forth' (75). There can be no end to an interpretative prose modelled on these lines, or indeed to its possible beginnings, since Derrida expatiates on the arbitrariness of both ends and beginnings as defining the 'edges' of a text (81–5). Indeed by the end of the third page concerned with the opening sentence 'We still have not exhausted its ambiguity', for 'living on can mean a reprieve or an after life, "life after life", or life after death, more life or more than life, and better, the state of suspension in which it's over—*and* over again, and you'll never have done with that suspension itself' (77). Derrida is quite right because of course any phrase unlimited by its context or co-text of situation can mean all that the dictionary and the native speaker and the interpretative critic, who is the one and has command of the other, says it can, at least to the critic himself who sets up this potentially closed circuit. Indeed Derrida's disseminatory, deconstructive method (of conducting a seminar as here) essentially depends on preventing any text—his own critical text or that of the author he purports to interpret—from imposing any such limitations on their own meaning or implications. Thus 'no meaning can be determined out of context, but no context permits saturation' (81). The text turns out to be Maurice Blanchot's *La Folie du jour* and *L'Arrêt de mort*, experimental works which allow, as we have argued, for this method, and Shelley's *Triumph of Life* (or purportedly so; but Derrida later announces (85) that it is not his intention to discuss it). Even the Blanchot text is something of a pre-text since in a later untypical gesture towards self-limitation, Derrida says he will refer to *L'Arrêt de mort* 'in order that my fragmentary discourse may remain somewhat intelligible, concrete, coherent' (104).

This freedom from the target-text spills over into a freedom from any limitation by reference to an implied speaker, either of the fictional text or of the interpretative discourse, for Derrida self-reflexively says that his own sentence 'But who's talking about living?', 'survives' its own speaker and 'does not require the presence or assistance of any party, male or female. The statement survives them a priori, lives on after them. Hence no context is saturable any more. No one inflection enjoys any absolute privilege, no meaning can be fixed or decided upon' (78). He attempts to prove his point, which essentially concerns the release of the sentence-meaning from any particular inferred intention on the part of a speaker, by printing it with different italicized emphases (i.e. different implied intonation contours). Thus even the illocutionary force of any sentence of the text must remain multiply determinable. Speech and writing of course differ in this respect, and Derrida could only make his point in the seminar by a recursive return to his own earlier utterance which the first time around, must have some intonation contour or other. Thus actors and speakers determine interpretations in so far as, unlike the reader, they have to choose the situations their intonations may be taken to imply : '"You are going to London" could have the illocutionary force of an assertion, a command, a request, a question, or an ironic comment on the fact that you are headed for Bristol.'[11]

However Derrida in his metadiscourse about discourse can go on to say truly enough that his (or rather the) question has really been set free from any particular context and hence from any such particular pragmatic implication. Derrida has in fact merely begun 'to reconstitute all sorts of corpora or contexts from which I might have taken it' (80 f.). Indeed the most general of these categories 'could be something like the language called French, or a family of languages more or less susceptible of translation of or into French' (81). Now if every sentence of a text (and presumably every sentence commenting on that sentence) can be freed from any determining intention or context, and seen in a setting as broad as this, then there are virtually no limits to interpretation (which in any case turns perpetually into an informal discourse on linguistics), and no constraints on what can either be relevantly or usefully said, except in the exercise of one's own virtuosity in the use of the language involved, which, as becomes clear in the sequel, is very considerable indeed in Derrida's case. Interpretation becomes performance.

Thus the text (and Derrida does not distinguish between the literary and the critical text—for him presumably the latter becomes as important as the former as it supplements it) no longer has any 'edges' or limitations (81). There is now 'a sort of overrun ['débordement'] that spoils all these boundaries and divisions'; we must extend the 'accredited concept' of the text (81 f.) which is 'no longer a finished corpus of writing, some content enclosed in a book or its margins, but a differential network, a fabric of traces referring endlessly to something other than itself, to other differential traces' (84). This will 'shock' those who believe in setting up limits or boundaries for the text : 'speech, life, the world, the real, history, and what not, every field of reference—to body or mind, conscious or unconscious, politics, economics, and so forth' (84). Derrida recognizes that there are some who might be inclined to 'blame difference as wrongful confusion', but attempts a rather unconvincing reassurance for them: 'it was never our wish to . . . transform the world into a library by doing away with all boundaries, all framework, all sharp edges . . . but that we ought rather to work on the theoretical and practical systems of these margins, these borders, once more, from the ground up. I shall not go into detail' (84). The peculiar lack of limitation on procedure in this particular piece does not help to reveal any such detail. One feels that deconstruction in this case has left a lot of disordered pieces just lying around, with very little of that constraining thematic construction of the type encountered in his more philosophical work. One might add that it is an invitation to play of a rather tired kind. For nearly all the possibilities he suggests for the meanings of his opening sentence, and for Blanchot, are far from new or interesting. His remarks on the possibilities of intonation are the feeble stuff of linguistic text-books dressed up in his own orotund style. The audience subjected to this performance may admire its virtuosity, but still wish to ask what the point of it is, not what some of the possible or remotely conceivable points may be. But if our illusions concerning the world are to be resisted, such impulses to tidy up may have to be refused.[12]

5.4 Norms for Interpretation

It is not simply disagreements among critics, but also the variations in the nature of the text, which deprive interpretation of many of the traditional assumptions by which it has claimed certainty. The diverse historical purposes of the text, from the mimetically transparent to the deliberately self-contradictory, make it difficult for the interpreter to claim that any critical language he may favour is given authority by virtue of its correspondence to the nature of nature, of literature, of literary convention, or even of language itself. The once confident relationship between critical language and its object has to be given up. But this confusion of literary and critical purposes tells us less about the ultimate nature of literature than about the varying philosophical assumptions with which we may approach the institution of literature and our talk about it.

One group of critics assumes or hopes that readers may come to agree about some relatively determinable meanings for texts, and their relationship to a stable world or world-like context. They have learnt enough from the Saussurean approach to linguistics to recognize that the ordering of nature in language may have been different, that a child for example may have learnt different distinctions between 'swan', 'duck', and 'goose' (or between epic elegy and ode at a later stage) had he belonged to a different community, i.e. that we impose orderings on nature and literature rather than vice versa. The similarities and differences which we learn and which give us control over the use of such concepts might have been exploited differently. Hence what we learn when we attempt to master the language with which we deal with reality, or the same language within the text, is, as we have insisted all along, a series of likeness-relations which are suitable for our purposes. They are

the preferred arrangement of some community, rather than something insisted on by nature itself. Nature does not mind how we make clusters from the vast array of similarities and differences we are able to discern in it; all that is required of such clusters is that they constitute a tolerable basis for further usage. The clusters are conventions; the similarity relations which concepts stand for are conventions.
None the less . . . in learning such conventions knowledge of nature is increased. At the end of his walk the child can identify swans in his environment, and hence expect of particular identified swans whatever his

community holds to be true or typical of them. By acquiring the communally sanctioned similarity relations, the child is able to apply the general knowledge of the community to particular situations in nature. The acquisition of culture gives the child a grip on experience.[1]

What the child learns about experience the critic learns similarly in working with the text. If he sees the text as embodying conventions (through the frameworks or schemas which realize them) he can attempt to discern a relatively stable hierarchy of semantic levels in it, all with their corresponding referential commitments, so that it is possible, not to make even finer distinctions about possible meanings within language, but, on the contrary, to make higher level generalizations about the text's relationship to the world. These generalizations form part of the social semiotic or conventions within which they are made, and also help to sustain it, simply by being accepted and used. Thus the *Iliad* may help us to form a concept of heroism, Shakespeare a concept of kingship, Wordsworth a sense of something immanent within nature, Lawrence a view of sexual relations, which are passed on into the community by interpretative statements.

The opposing group believe as we have seen that such closures or generalizations are unsubtle in their approach to the language of the text and ideologically suspect. The meaning of the text is indeterminate and its power or energy or interest may only be sustained by keeping it so. This willed indeterminacy may depend on the ingenuity and subtlety of the critic, as he attempts to upset the 'preferred arrangements' of the community. The different styles of such readings may in the end be determined by the individual psychology and beliefs of the reader, but they also make their way in the community by virtue of his institutional authority or claims to representative status. For the circumstances in which subjectivist criticism is tolerated are in fact just as well defined as those in which, say, moral criticism is possible.[2]

Richard Rorty argues convincingly that these apparently antithetical interpretative positions stem from different philosophical traditions (not surprisingly so, since it is at the philosophical level that they have at base to be defended or attacked).[3] The one tradition is Kantian, seeing truth as a matter of relationship (correspondence) to things represented, and making scientific enquiry the centre of concern, since it seems to be tied most rigorously to the observations which support such correspondence. Within this Kantian framework we can attack specific problems and make progress. Our general world-picture is thus made up of an increasing supply of empirical certainties or high probabilities. And of course it would be good for humanistic endeavours, like history and literary interpretation, if this were the case, since they could then claim to provide knowledge rather than opinion. The critical tradition would help us approach, asymptotically maybe, to the truth of the meaning of the text and its relationship to the world.

The counter to this position (which Derrida and others are quite right in asserting to have long been the established one) is post-Hegelian. It asserts that what we accept as the truth is in fact only the latest in a long series of interpretations of past experience, and that our acceptance of any such latest position is not determined so much by its empirical well-foundedness as by its general coherence. Within this broad historical view, we may be brought to see that even science, and the Kantian philosophical discourse associated with it, cannot be given any peculiar position of privilege. 'La grammatologie doit déconstruire tout ce qui lie le concept et les normes de la scientificité à l'ontothéologie, au logocentrisme, au phonologisme. C'est un travail immense et interminable.'[4]

If we look at the matter with the hindsight of historical perspective, we can see that these types of discourse didn't really live up to the Kantian ideal, but utilized all sorts of metaphors, myths, models, and ideological frameworks which, once we are aware of them, make science and philosophy and interpretation seem much less progressive, more controlled by provisional historical frameworks, and hence far more relativistic than we may like to believe. That is to say, they are not part of a network of co-operative enterprises which are commensurable with one another.[5] Of course Sophocles, Chaucer, and I will share a very large number of beliefs of an everyday character. But their notions of God, slavery, madness, poetry, and so on will be rather different from mine, and the differences here, despite the apparent communality of belief embodied in the common word, will turn on some quite general characteristics of their conceptual schemas or world-view. It is variations in such concepts that are both significant and ultimately irreconcilable : both Arnold and Marx write about 'class' but with different assumptions and to different ends. It is the history of the many problematic concepts involved in our controlling frameworks of belief that leads one to assert that succeeding philosophers, commentators, scientists, and literary critics may resemble one another in their activities, but they cannot solve such problems or provide definitions that will do once and for all. They are involved in a perpetually evolving dialectical tradition, in which earlier positions are perpetually rewritten, or deconstructed, or sometimes even revived, by individuals.

All these arguments have their effect at the level of the text.

Derrida thus denies that language ever attains to that certainty of reference ('presence') that the Kantians demand. For all such claims will break down when sceptically viewed. They will so break, partly because, as we have seen in discussing metaphors, Derrida's criteria for success in matching texts to the world are pitched absurdly high, as Charles Altieri points out :

his arguments for textual indeterminacy rest on two main claims: that only names or uniquely referring descriptions can securely make publicly assessable claims to be meaningful since only names can serve a purely denotative function and provide pictures of facts, and that all texts that express desire displace this pure naming fiction by requiring multiple decoding frameworks and thus disseminating an endless chain of commentaries deferring and differing from the now irrecoverable original act of referring. In his work the emotive-referential dichotomy takes the form that there are only two types of discourse—those that picture facts and are publicly verifiable by non-linguistic means or those that depend on patterns of association among auditors which have no public object or determinable function.[6]

It is thus a scepticism concerning reference that makes it at all too plausible for Derridans to propose an alternative meaning or use for the text. If language use lacks the stability of Kantian correspondence, then it may indeed be seen as perpetually self-referring, or as simply disseminating meanings. Since no particular view of the world need tie us down, it is argued that the way is open for associations of meaning which would otherwise look peculiarly arbitrary and subjective. But their arbitrariness is supposed not to matter, since at no point are they going to be called to a stop by any 'privileged' sense of a situation, directly related to or even like that of the world. No appeal from text to world is allowed. We are trapped within the text and within our own interpretation of it, as Derrida argues:

Si la lecture ne doit pas se contenter de redoubler le texte, elle ne peut légitimement transgresser le texte vers autre chose que lui, vers un référent (réalité métaphysique, historique, psycho-biographique, etc.) ou vers un signifié hors texte dont le contenu pourrait avoir lieu, aurait pu avoir lieu hors de la langue, c'est-à-dire, au sens que nous donnons ici à ce mot, hors de l'écriture en générale.[7]

We are always 'within language': we cannot transcend or get beyond it, and we are only capable, by definition, of taking those paths within it available to our particular culture or epoch. Further, if all we say has neither certain foundation in correspondence, nor stopping-point in any arrest to the play of differences, all our interpretations are rewritings. We are not trying to tell the truth about an object, whether as text or as language, since there is no bedrock of fact on which to base it (since all facts are themselves interpretations). Any attempt to specify such a foundation is doomed to failure since it will simply be the further extension of a type of language game which there is every reason to distrust. And even a sceptical deconstructive analysis 'can never have the final word because its insights are inevitably couched in a rhetoric which is open to further deconstructive reading.'[8]

Of course all philosophers and interpreters do rewrite in so far as they refer back to and criticize their predecessors. They address the same problems and texts, and they even claim to make progress, by pointing out earlier contradictions and aporias. All philosophical arguments and all interpretations extend a play of differences by definition—they differ from their predecessors and from the canonical texts which they rewrite.

Thus much interpretative activity is caught in a position in which it purports to correspond to a text, but will always in fact differ from it and displace it. We might say that we think that a text says or implies, 'the same as . . .' in, say, French. A translation may be thought to be as close as we can get. But as we have already seen, the words we use in French will have different implications from those we use in English. They occupy and lead off to different points in the conceptual space of the reader. (Or within the 'langue' of the reader inferred as a model from his 'parole'.) We may declare the meaning in the language of the text as synonymously as possible. The objection we have recorded has even greater force, because the paraphrase words clearly occupy a different 'position' in the language. And so explanations of meaning of this type are hardly ever completely substitutable for the original expression. To this extent indeed a line of poetry 'means what it says' and nothing else.

However, I derive from these considerations not a Derridan scepticism which licenses a free play of the text, but a view of the relationship between text and explanation or interpretation as a pragmatic matter (like advice). Its force and meaning come from the force and meaning and *justification* of certain further moves within language; or, to continue in our return to our starting-point—the *choice* of implications for the text. Thus the logic of interpretation should not concern itself with the problems of conveying the exact meaning in other words or of pointing to any exact correspondence of the text to the external world : as we have seen, should those exist they could only be recognized. Interpretative paraphrase will in any case rewrite the correspondence, and depend on likeness rather than specific reference. Interpretative exactitude is *ex hypothesi* impossible.

We are concerned in interpretation with the logic and justification of the institutional practice of putting into circulation critical interpretative paraphrases of texts instead of the text, for certain purposes which will always deviate to some degree from those of the text. This is because interpretation will always, for Derridans and non-Derridans, favour some implication of the text, which it is thought *useful* for the reader to know.[9] I argue then that the study of interpretation should be the study of the pragmatic and ideological commitments of typical or culturally favoured types of implication for texts, including those which relate the text to the world, and of the logic by which such implications are derived, and the grounds advanced for them. I exemplify this in Chapter 6.

The problem then becomes, for Derridans and non-Derridans alike, whether within this perpetual interpretative play of difference and paraphrase, even when it is governed by plausible implication (such as we have tried to demonstrate for metaphor, the codes and indeed for historical reference) there are any grounds which can place any acceptable limitations upon what can be said. We wish to know the norms whereby some choices of implication may seem to be more worthwhile than others. I write here of the actual practice of interpretative criticism, as it is; of course one can, as I think Derrida does, *prescriptively define* the literary text as that kind of text which puts such norms into abeyance, when he speaks of ' "literary" convention, the suspension of "normal" contexts, the context of everyday conversational usage or of writing legitimatized by law.'[10] But this is I think merely prescriptive, and paradoxically of course proposes a different set of 'norms' for interpretation.

We are thus led to reply to Derrida and those who think like him, that their dismissal of our usual criteria for objectivity serves an ideological end—that of excluding referential talk, or reference to privileged transcendental signifieds, such as those involved in moral discourse. 'Objectivity' may indeed be a relativistic matter, and often uncertain, but not to the crippling extent that they would have us believe. For the privileging of certain interpretative concepts (like those of character *or* of free play) is a matter for established procedures within a model of inquiry, of our agreed practices within professional groups. An attack on privileged concepts or our notions of objectivity is thus ultimately an attack on those groups, and on the ends for which they accept paradigms in interpretation, or 'modes of valid procedure for pedagogic use', as Barnes put it with reference to the repertoire of paradigms used by scientists.[11]

In adopting any particular set of norms for interpretation then, we may well be aware of their varying descriptive or factual adequacy (as Austin pointed out, saying that France is 'hexagonal' is perfectly acceptable for some purposes, and not for others[12]). It is similarly easier to relate *Middlemarch* to the Reform Bill or to nineteenth-century attitudes to mythological research than it is to relate it to some Freudian allegory, since the norms for historical correspondence are more widely accepted and better understood than those for Freudian unconscious motivation and symbolism.

I thus propose a form of contextual relativism. For it is particularly in the light of Derrida's fundamental critique, that we can see from the past conflicting practices of criticism, and from our study of metaphor and code, that the text alone under-determines its own context of interpretation (or, in other words, is not sufficient alone to help us decide on a context for interpretation). Our perception of the text's implications and willingness to mediate them is thus inevitably subject to non-textual interpretative norms. When a relativist theory of this kind is joined to a theory of consensus like that advanced in T. S. Kuhn's philosophy of science, which emphasizes the institutional context in which literature is interpreted, then 'the reaction of others to an interpretation becomes a test of its value'.[13] None the less, even if the interpretation of the text must thus logically depend upon our agreements concerning its meaning and implications, it still remains the case that the way in which we arrive at those agreements will depend on our procedures for *justifying* what we say, our ability to give reasons for our judgement even if this is 'not a matter of any special relation between ideas or words and objects [in our case, texts] but of conversation, of social practice.'[14] I thus attempted earlier to defend the 'social practice' of making an audience aware of the historical context from which a text derives or of which it may speak. This shows that even the relativist will attempt to adjudicate between frameworks on grounds of value (in this case the usefulness of remaining aware of historical facts, perhaps on the over-confident ground that knowledge is *ipso facto* likely to be of more use than ignorance, or that respect for what we take to be facts may be in some ways 'better' than fantasy concerning history).

Rorty, from whom I quoted above, goes on to say that 'We understand knowledge when we understand the social justifications of belief, and thus have no need to view it as accuracy of representation'.[15] My argument parallels his. In view of what we have said about implication and paraphrase, and in accepting the sceptical force of much deconstructivist argument, we cannot accept a model for interpretation which depends upon the notions of 'accuracy of representation' of the text's (intended or other) meanings or of its referential commitments. No such absolute correspondence is possible. As we shall see in the following chapter, interpretation always thus leaves us with choices which require justification in the manner outlined above : and these justifications will ultimately turn on the norms accepted by particular interpretative groups. These change in history, in a manner very little different from that which Kuhn describes for 'Normal' and 'Revolutionary' science. Workable norms are discarded when they are felt to contain anomalies. Thus to take a simple example, those who accepted that Vergil may have been divinely inspired to foretell the coming of Christ in his Fourth Eclogue were succeeded by those who didn't. Both groups had workable norms for the interpretation of the implications of the text, but the mode of their justification changed. For even if the Christian allegorization 'works', it can be pointed out that it depends upon a conventional justification (the divine inspiration of the virtuous pagan) which has since been rejected. If we wish to reject the notion of divine intervention and stick to what Vergil could have known in his time without it, the Christian interpretation looks much less likely.[16]

If the above arguments are accepted, we find that the theory of interpretation, along with its methods and justifications, is itself part of an historical process, as each interpreter (like the writer of this argument) sees himself as an institutionally backed contributor to an historical process of understanding in the evolution of which conceptual frameworks for interpretation have changed, and will continue to do so.[17]

If Richard Rorty is right, Derrida would have at least a partial reply to my defence of historical, mimetical, or moral criticism and deconstruction as all workable norm-governed types of interpretation. He would simply prefer that at this historical juncture we did not produce the first three of these, and would like to see what the world would be like if we changed these norms and paradigms for others. For him any accord with the norms of common sense simply isn't interesting; reference in particular is not really important. Derrida just wishes that we didn't have any views on such matters at all, rather as the atheist wishes that people didn't bother to write theology.[18] God does not exist and we shouldn't waste time talking about him; the Kantian view of the world has equally given itself up as hostage to an impossible myth of presence and should not be pursued. As Rorty puts it, Derrida 'is suggesting how things might look if we did not have Kantian philosophy built into the fabric of our intellectual life, as his predecessors suggested how things might look if we didn't have religion built into the fabric of our moral life'.[19]

This is a perfectly possible preference, but in our terms it has to substitute one set of norms for another. Even Derridan deconstructive readings will have to observe some interpretative conventions; as anyone who has read very many of them will be forced to conclude they do. Editors of collections of such works have little difficulty in discerning a family resemblance among them.[20] They thus advance historically upon Kantian or traditional types of interpretation by themselves observing the value norms of scepticism and to a degree, of subjectivism, that we have discerned within them. Their justification is thus also ultimately a pragmatic one. Scepticism and the free play it licenses are supposed to be more worthwhile activities within the institutions of interpretation, than the subservience to the transcendental signified of the previous consensual system.

This sceptical approach is indeed of value for a number of reasons whose force we will come to appreciate more fully when we come to discuss ideology. But they should be summarized here, lest our discussion of deconstruction be thought too negative. Firstly, the Derridan approach makes us wary of a too easy acceptance of the norms of our own practice, particularly as regards mimesis, in so far as this is ideologically suspect or forecloses on the implications of the text.

Secondly, as we saw in looking at de Man, we are forced to look more closely at the self-controverting complexity and varying unreliability of the supposedly normative or realist text. We are helped to see how the text itself may exploit or even subvert the Kantian conventions; or unwittingly run itself into contradiction (this will prove of great importance in ideological interpretation).

Thirdly, deconstructive practices may prevent us from allowing an overconfident, unifying view of language as a system of representation to impose a particular ideology or an idealizing unity on the text. We saw how in 'Billy Budd' no single frame of reference was possible; and so the text itself is fissured. This type of consideration has even more force for those texts which are not themselves unified, like *The Waste Land*, which critics still attempt to force into a thematic unity.

For fourthly, the text itself may be disunified or fissured by precisely those aporias or contradictions that the deconstructive method is peculiarly able to reveal. That is, quite apart from the general theoretical claims of deconstruction as a universally appropriate mode of interpretation, there may be a separate modified claim, that it is peculiarly apt to certain types of avant-garde or experimental text, which are themselves caught up in a dialectical relationship with the Kantian 'normal' text.

The present practice of interpretation, in so far as critics are aware of the structuralist revolution, and its consequences, is thus itself caught up in a dialectic between normal and abnormal, coherence-conferring and deconstructive approaches to the text. (This is neatly symbolized in Derrida's work by his putting certain concepts he is attacking 'sous rature' ('under erasure') so that they both are and are not there ('inscrivant violemment dans le texte ce qui tentait de le commander du dehors' ('inserting violently within the text that which was trying to command it from outside')[21]). Thus one of the main functions of the distinct groups of critics attracted to each side of this dialectic is to criticize the other—'no constructors, no deconstructors'.[22] The two groups thus observe not only certain conditions of mental hygiene (logical conditions of interpretation) but also make ideological choices concerning the significance of their work.

Indeed one of the benefits of the current shift toward indeterminacy in interpretation may well be that it brings to the fore the fact that in inevitably observing some norm or other, the interpreter is so committed. It is only in periods like our own in which the norms or paradigms for interpretation are changing that he is acutely aware of this. We see ourselves as interpreting for particular purposes and thus need to defend ourselves as pursuing values which really are in question. The deconstructive urge may thus well be one which refuses subservience to established order, as the free play of the text breaks with the conventional wisdom institutionalized in everyday uses of language.

Subjectivist interpretation may, as a corollary, demonstrate the freedom or creativity of the critic, his willingness to let his writing compete with that of the text.[23] Such ends lead to a series of preferences within the literary tradition. A deconstructive critic may well be expected to celebrate the divided romantic creative imagination, as opposed to the ordered neoclassic subordination to universals; or attracted to the text as determined by conflicting creative intentions, as in much avant-garde writing; or as opposed to enclosed forms, hence the appeal to the fragmentary unfinished work; or as obviously fictional or confusingly 'factoid' as opposed to naturalistic, and so on.

As these choices are made and more and more students are inducted into the anti-normal norms of deconstructive interpretation, so there has taken place a large change in English studies.[24] We cease to see literature as interesting for its reinforcement of social or moral attitudes in a historical context, but as problematic in relation to them.

Literature is thus being understood, taught, and hence interpreted, both as a means of understanding and criticizing experience in an Arnoldian fashion, allied to those systems of education which introduce the reader to a stable traditional system of culture and history, and also more subversively and more strategically, as the locus of a linguistic play which indeed may give pleasure simply as such, but which may also remind us of our uncertainty, as it perpetually refuses, or pretends to refuse, to articulate the world for us in the way that the traditionalists might claim. The post-structuralist and deconstructive movement has thus made a distinctive and original contribution to the study of the relationship between literature and belief, and it is to this that I now turn.

6.1 Ideology and Opposition

It is a consequence of our argument so far that there can be no single epistemologically sound mode of interpretation which is applicable to all texts. This is because the texts themselves will be more or less epistemologically well founded in their correspondence to the external world, or may deliberately confuse any such correspondence, and further because the text will generate implications which themselves may cause an epistemological uncertainty in the interpreter. There can no more be universal norms for these implications than there can be for the texts which give rise to them.

We are thus left, as we noted at the conclusion of the last chapter, with a number of choices within the institutions we have for the reading and interpretation of literature. Within these varying institutional contexts we decide what we are using the text for.[1] In some such contexts such as those of biblical interpretation or the law, procedures and the ends they may serve are closely defined for particular groups. Indeed, any radical doubts about the rules of construction are discouraged.[2] This is hardly the case for literary interpretation, whose academic context of free enquiry feeds scepticism. What is more, the interests of those to whom interpretations are offered are far less well defined, and may even have to be located (as in the giving of good advice) before interpretation can become effective.[3]

The norms of interpretation thus operate within institutional contexts for diverse ends. But I wish now to ask how far they may have an ideological or political character. We shall find that no interpretation is ideologically innocent, even if, for interesting reasons that we will come to discuss, it may pretend to be. For it is the apparent naturalness of the norms we share with others, of the literary tradition we consider important, and of our educational formation (the pedagogical methods of particular institutions) which can prevent us from considering their ideological implications. It is thus the attempt to reveal ideology by and in interpretation that will be our chief concern.

The notion of ideology itself is a complex one. It can have a descriptive sense which presupposes a neutral observer: as when the anthropologist describes a 'cultural system'—its kinship-relations, its scientific and religious beliefs, its legal institutions, and so on, and their interaction. However, most of us think of ideology as it may operate within an individual member of a group as an overall 'framework of belief' or 'world picture' giving rise to moral norms which typically guide his actions. The description of this framework would be a more indirect and selective enterprise than that of the anthropologist. It would in particular wish to give some indication of the way in which beliefs cohere (their interrelations which make the individual wish to sustain them as a whole). In an 'explicit' ideology this coherence is a matter of some importance—hence say the relationship of theology to Christian practice, or Marxism to certain types of Socialism. Also relevant here would be the centrality of such beliefs, the way they relate to basic issues, of life, death, work, sexuality, and so on, and as a corollary the degree of resistance the individual offers against relinquishing them.

I use the word 'belief' rather than 'ideology' by design, as ideology is typically thought of as somehow being more than a framework of belief, in that it is wedded to a programme for action in the light of a *model* of the nature of human society. Thus Lenin urges that the 'independent ideology' of the labour movement is 'the set of those attitudes and beliefs which would best enable the workers to reconstruct society in their own interest'.[4]

It is ideology in this latter sense that liberals once thought they could do without and made them feel that ideology has a pejorative sense. But a positive need for ideology may nevertheless remain, if we wish to participate in frameworks of belief that make life 'meaningful' for us and help us to feel that we are part of a culture.[5] And political actions, goals, and ideals obviously arise most forcefully out of such a framework. It has been forcefully argued by the Frankfurt School, that ideological commitments of this kind also carry with them, implicitly or explicitly, a reliance upon the legitimacy of particular social institutions and practices, and of the power relations they sustain. Thus according to Habermas and others, an ideology is a world picture which stabilizes or legitimizes domination.

All this I think amounts to a fairly common-sense, if oversimpli-fied, notion of ideology in its non-pejorative sense. It is a notion however which has been made considerably more complex by a predominantly Marxist line of argument which suggests that the way in which individuals stand in relation to such ideological beliefs is open to criticism.[6] They are thought to be deluded, and to involve a 'false consciousness'. As Geuss points out, they may simply be epistemologically inadequate (the Gods do not in fact exist; or a subgroup may falsely take its interests to be the interests of the group as a whole)[7] or they may function in some undesirable way (e.g. legitimize the unfair oppression of one group by another) or they may be held for some bad or unacknowledged motive—they may arise in the wrong way. Thus I may have views which arise from and 'express' my class position (and thus never have considered properly the interests of others).[8] The real problem here is not so much the causal manner in which my belief came about, interesting though that may be, as its undesirability or inappropriacy on other grounds.

It is this critical approach to the relationship of the individual and the literary texts he produces to ideological belief with which we will be chiefly concerned in what follows.[9] I think it may be helpful, if still a little elementary, if we remind ourselves of some of the typical features of obvious or overt ideological positions, like those of the Roman Catholic or Marxist or Democratic Liberal. They all attempt, more or less coercively, to be of universal appeal. Ideologies are in competition. The first two have a peculiar certainty about the truth revealed to them, and indeed about the direction of history, towards revolution or salvation. They are thus also teleological, setting before us a goal, an ideal state of earthly or heavenly society. They are programmatic in the sense mentioned above. The end-states they aim at, including that of a liberal democracy, are often justified by the freedom which we are expected to enjoy within the society they project. Paradoxically enough, the process of obtaining this freedom within history may involve a high degree of obedience to authority and extinction of self-will.

Thus the actions of a Marxist should perhaps be in accord with the 'laws' of the progressive tendency which he discerns within society. The Roman Catholic is expected to place his trust in his Church's teaching of a divinely revealed truth in seeking salvation. The liberal is expected to believe that the free competition of beliefs and interests among men will conduce to the general good in the long run and so on. Thus ideologists tend to serve competing interests within society, and often enough to do so through the institutions which claim to preserve and represent them—the Church, the political party, the 'democratic process', and so on.

Within this perspective the institution of literature (which includes the writing, printing, and distribution of literary works, as well as our discourse about it, which may involve a parallel writing, printing, and distribution) may not be seen as autonomous.[10] For our discourse within and about literature may be seen not only to express ideology in the senses we have described, but also to serve or to contradict such ideological ends. Indeed all works of literature are at definable distances from them. We can see how the *Divine Comedy* and *Paradise Lost* may serve religious ends, and less clearly perhaps how *Tom Jones*, *David Copperfield*, or *The Waste Land* may serve political ones.[11] Even those discourses not explicitly related to external authority will have an ideological significance in so far as they project a view of the nature of human beings. For ideologists also claim, I think, to be able to say something quite definite about human nature or human values. They thus invade the sphere of moral discourse with which many are inclined to think of as somehow autonomous. Man may be born to serve God, his value in society may consist in his labour, he may be seen as basically competitive or self-reliant, or as basically fraternal and egalitarian, or none or all of these at once.[12]

Ideologies thus tend to promote certainties of a kind we have not encountered before in our argument, and thus may lead to a direct confrontation between the beliefs of the interpreter and those supposedly asserted by the text. We may be able to clarify some of these central themes, of the appeal to an historical context, of political ends, of freedom and of human nature, if we introduce at this stage an example.

The controversy over Camus's *La Peste* (published in June 1947) shows how these oppositions arise. The story centres round the activities of Dr Rieux. Rats appear in the city of Oran, but the authorities act too late to prevent them from spreading the plague, and the City is cut off from the rest of the world. The inhabitants (and Rieux in particular, who is separated from his wife) suffer most from their sense of isolation. Many try to ignore the existence of the plague. But the Jesuit Father Paneloux preaches a violent sermon on it (and thus himself interprets Camus's text theologically) as a just punishment. Later, after he has witnessed the death of a small boy, he gives a second, less confident sermon. After six months the fury of the plague diminishes (it is not known whether it was successfully resisted). The town gradually returns to normal, and the book ends with the revelation that Dr Rieux himself was its author, and has written to bear witness to the violence and injustice imposed on his town. But the plague will come again.

This very crude summary of the plot fails to do justice to the complexity of Camus's narrative; in particular its teasing relationship between documentary realism and symbol. But *La Peste* was perceived as having these larger implications, as an allegorical account of the condition of France under German occupation, and of the need for resistance (under the guise of Rieux's *équipes sanitaires*). This was in accord with Camus's own view as expressed in a letter to Roland Barthes.[13] The theme of the separation of Oran from the rest of the world recalled that of France in 1940 to 1944, and there were thought to be confirming details for this, i.e. a series of motivated similarities between the world of the text and that of a particular historical period. The cinemas which would be closed in a plague are not closed in the book, nor were they under the occupation, the Arabs do not figure in the book much, and this indicated that the book is a fable about metropolitan France.[14] Once this version of verisimilitude combined with an allegorical parallel is proposed, it is possible to criticize the novel for the political position implied by its symbolism. Thus René Étiemble, seizing on the Oran/France parallel, went so far as to attack the book (in Sartre's *Les Temps modernes*) for failing to indicate any subsequent reform of the medical services, as an indication that political reform was needed in post-war France. Philip Thody makes the full assent to defending the book as an ideological allegory. He argues that Tarrou's and Rieux's struggle against the plague, frequently referred to as 'l'abstraction', is Camus's own fight against the abstract logic of the Marx-ist—Hegelian view of history and against totalitarianism in all its forms.

Translated into political terms [the book] is a plea for toleration and liberalism, an argument for Popper's 'piecemeal social engineering' against Lenin's idea of violent revolution followed by a complete reorganisation of society . . . *La Peste* is an attempt to show that totalitarianism inevitably relies on mass murder to impose its rule and therefore can only increase human misery. It also points out that there are other, more modest, ways of trying to improve society.[15]

Étiemble and Thody clearly wished to see the book as licensing their political assertions, and hence as having an ideological use. Most significantly, they wished to see it as a conscious political utterance, as a particular type of speech act conditioned by a particular historical situation, a 'plea', and as asking what particular types of free action are possible within that situation. They thus take up two of the key positions within ideology as we have sketched it.

It might be thought that there is an alternative mode of interpretation of *La Peste* available, and I wish to sketch it here, as it conflicts, or appears to conflict, with the political approach. It is less concerned to map social structure on to political structure than to concentrate upon the moral concerns of the individual. Thus the novel may be concerned with moral issues with no clear political overtones, such as the limits of the freedom of men like Rieux to resist evil. This view of the novel would accord with that of David Caute, when he says that 'the novel or play as a structure, as a genre, tends to affirm the individual and deny the society. That is why the most successful committed novels are critiques of the social system rather than hymns of praise to its alternative'.[16] Hence indeed, such interpreters would say, Camus's own emphasis on revolt, rather than upon revolution, which requires the specification of an end-state. This issue was a bone of contention between him and Sartre.[17] If this is the case, then a large part of the tradition of the novel would be taken to support a particular view of the value of the individual and of our moral discourse about it. This has been constantly affirmed in philosophical terms by Camus himself, and its affinity with political liberalism (from Stendhal on indeed) is clear. But this relationship of political to moral discourse is a controversial one to which we must return.

It may well be that some correspondence rules would help us to adjudicate between these various interpretations of Camus by showing that one or another of them have an adequate interpretation of more of the book, or of its symbolic mode of narration i.e. of its implications (without of course thereby being inconsistent with other parts). But the point I wish to make here is rather simpler. In the types of interpretation we have described, the context of situation ('utterance') of the text is specified in such a way to make it relevant to a particular historical situation. The interpretation, as we have urged all along, mediates the relationship of the text to the world. In doing this it has to take a particular view of the co-text as licensing these moves, and the typical way for this to be done is via mimesis or verisimilitude. The interpretations of *La Peste* cited ultimately depend on a notion of the mimetic commitments of the novel, so that the world within the work and that without it may confront one another.

This confrontation can be given considerable weight and significance, as we can see if we look at the attitude to prose fiction expressed by Sartre at roughly the same time. He argues that literary objects are used to communicate between members of a society, to create a social group of readers in which, as he puts it, the reader is called into a society of communicating freedoms akin to Kant's Kingdom of Ends, so that in writing, the writer expresses his freedom in addressing the freedom of another:

The writer has chosen to reveal the world and particularly to reveal men to other men so that they may assume full responsibility before the object which has been made bare. It is assumed that no one is ignorant of the law because there is a code and the law is written down; thereafter you are free to violate it, but you know the risks you run. Similarly, the function of the writer is to act in such a way that nobody can be ignorant of the world and that nobody may say that he is innocent of what it's all about.[18]

This is, in its appeal to responsibility, a wildly optimistic view of the moral function of literature, and yet its cognitive base seems assured by that relationship between recognition and evidence which we argued for earlier, and which underlies all cases of 'realism'. We can see what Sartre is after if we read a single sentence from Orwell: 'that scene stays in my mind as one of my pictures of Lancashire; the dumpy shawled women, with their sacking aprons and their heavy black clogs, kneeling in the cindery mud and the bitter wind, searching eagerly for scraps of coal'.[19] If we accept the truth of this description, which we can confirm within a norm-governed procedure by looking for what counts within it as independent evidence, then we may, as Sartre urges, ask as 'free' readers whether any human being should be brought to behave in this way. We might indeed feel 'responsible' in so far as we can persuade ourselves that anything like this still happens. We see through idiosyncratic pictorial features (such as the possibility that not all the women Orwell saw were 'dumpy', 'shawled', or 'eager') to the basic social fact. But such facts are not usually open to the simple recognition of the eyewitness or to direct inspection. They then depend on our privileging other types of 'historical' texts which we take as confirming the world/text relationship. And our notion of the historical text itself depends upon its relationship to what we accept as 'factual evidence'.[20] We use our accepted notion of history to delimit the context of the text; and in doing this we have to be aware of the deconstructive arguments we analysed earlier. For history itself is a narrative construct, and it is up to us to decide what parts of these we are willing to be deconstructively sceptical of. We remain within a network of texts, all of which are in varying relationship to our notion of factual adequacy. We shall see in what follows that it is indeed our attitude to this kind of realism, or historical adequacy in the text, that governs ideological interpret-ation.

However, a Sartrean trust in the mimetic adequacy of the text allows the relationship of literature to ideology to depend on a rather simple model. The text is judged, like the facts of history which it simulates, from an ideological or moral point of view. Such judgements ask: does the text confirm or contradict the beliefs independently held by the interpreter? This relationship is so logical and so obvious that academics in particular tend to forget or even suppress it except when it is brought to light by the censor. For the beliefs of others as expressed in the text are or are not in accord with our own.[21] I shall call this the *oppositional model*. In using this model I of course parallel the Marxist model of contest or dialectic between the legitimation of ideology (by a dominant class) and contestation (on which see below). I would only add that there is no necessity for the ideology to be that of a dominant class. One could for example contest the beliefs of a subgroup or subculture, religious or political.

It has recently been pointed out that the way in which such potential conflicts have been resolved in academic interpretation is unsatisfactory. They had, I think, usually been resolved in two ways: by a liberal argument with respect to belief and by a deflection of the political import of the text on to the more neutral ground of moral criticism. Thus a dissonance of belief between reader and text could be resolved by an argument that went at its simplest like this: of course literary works can express beliefs (and indeed usually assert them, as we can see by reading Wordsworth, Jane Austen, or Tolstoy, who are prone to make generalizations).[22] But in those cases in which we do not share the author's belief, we could at least be thought to be discovering what they were, and thus assimilate them to a general mode of tolerance. These attitudes found an influential focus in the work of Richards and Eliot. The former claimed that 'intellectual belief' could be suspended, in Coleridgean fashion, in favour of emotional integration. Thus 'the fact that Donne [in his sonnet 'At the round earth's imagined corners'] gave both forms of belief to those ideas [Resurrection] need not, I think, prevent a good reader from giving the fullest emotional belief while withholding intellectual belief.'[23] Eliot also takes up this point about emotion and suggests that even where there is no 'great philosophy' behind poetry as in

> As flies to wanton boys are we to the Gods;
> They kill us for their sport

it may still express 'some permanent human impulse'.[24] He also believes that 'belief and disbelief may be suspended', indeed 'that is the advantage of a coherent system of dogma and morals like the Catholic; it stands apart, for understanding and dissent even without belief, for the single individual who propounds it.'[25]

The often complementary deflecting argument goes like this: in any case, we can prefer in interpretation arguments which emphasize or privilege values of a psychological or moral kind ('the eternal human heart', 'irony', etc.) which are thought to transcend our ideological involvement in problems of belief. This type of consensus was obviously of advantage in academic contexts, in which students from different backgrounds could be asked to co-operate in a politically neutral and yet morally elevating enterprise. It is precisely these assumptions concerning the liberal model and its associated languages for interpretation which are now under attack.[26]

For critical theorists have recently urged that such manœuvres themselves reflect an insidious 'dominant ideology' in interpretation which is designed to defuse the real relationships between literature, belief, history, society, and the interpreter. Far from conspiring to hide the ideology within the text we should aim to reveal it, and success in such an enterprise will depend in part in disturbing these 'liberal' or 'empiricist' or 'common-sense' norms. This disturbance has been to some degree achieved by the deconstructive hostility to the privileged 'transcendental signifieds' of traditional criticism, and by the recent revival of a Marxist theoretical criticism. I wish in the following sections to look more closely at some of these attempts to disturb some of the current norms for interpretation, which attack not only the liberal consensus, but also the Sartrean norms of realism on which they seem to be based.

6.2 Hidden Ideology

We might begin our investigation of the questions raised at the end
of the last section by returning to consider some of the issues raised
in the work of Barthes, reported earlier. He attempted to show, in
S/Z, how the text exploits codes which reflect the negotiation of
ideological assumptions between text and reader. They are made to
seem 'natural', whereas they are really, and more sinisterly,
'entièrement livresque' and part of the dominant bourgeois ideology.[1] We might raise a rather simple objection to this type of
argument, by agreeing that the codes Barthes discusses were indeed
implicit in the text, but denying, since the reader can as easily
adopt as superior a notion of mimetic adequacy as Barthes himself,
that we need necessarily be taken in by such artificial conventions,
whether in literature or in advertising. But whatever the facts may
be concerning our ability to resist such blandishments, with or
without the benefits of critical interpretation, Barthes would be
correct in pointing out that within any given historical period,
everyday language and literature, advertising, photography, and so
on, do convey these hidden ideological assumptions, precisely at the
point at which they seem most transparent. It is indeed an
important function of critical interpretation to make us aware of
their ideological nature.

Thus for most of us a certain way of thinking about sex differences
was, until a while ago, 'natural'. Distinctions were encoded in the
language that men and women did not dispute, having no external
perspective from which to challenge them.[2] But they became much
less transparent and less acceptable once they were seen to support
distinctions and differences which had become objectionable. And
so the language system itself has had to give at certain points (for
example, by the insertion of 'Ms' into the system 'Mr', 'Mrs',
'Miss'): 'we are aware of the connection between language and
ideology in these instances because the position of women in the
social structure and ideology is currently in transition.'[3]

Our awareness of ideology is thus most clearly focused when it is
foregrounded by historical change or discovery. This has always
been the case, for example in Julien Sorel's immense sensitivity to
the language of liberalism and conservatism in *Le Rouge et le Noir*, or
Frédéric Moreau's to the changing rhetoric of 1848 in *L'Éducation
sentimentale*. However, there may be far less of significance to be

revealed within literature, where such frameworks of belief have
long been at issue, than in media like advertising and television,
where there may well be strong motives for disguising them (or at
least in advertising, for working by indirection). As Barthes pointed
out, the advertiser's phrase 'Sécrétaire, je veux être impéccable'
reflects a whole series of assumptions concerning the subordination
of women : 'a whole ethos of acceptance of masculine prerogatives'
in the presentation of the work of a secretary as self-abnegatory, a
role in which one can always 'exhibit' clothes'.[4]

Catherine Belsey deals similarly with perfume advertising.[5] Here
different smells, which are not all that easily discriminated in fact,
have to be artificially differentiated by the advertiser. He does this
by associating them in his advertisement with a 'social meaning', so
that 'the product becomes a signifer of specific cultural or ideological
values'.[6] This is seen by the way in which different perfumes are
aimed at different types of women, from the daydreamer of the
romantic film to the 'liberated' woman. Once we are aware of this
we can see how the advertisement is a 'source of information about
ideology, about semiotics, about the cultural and photographic
codes of our society'.[7]

What advertisements thus reveal in fact are the norms for their
own interpretation, and it is a separate question whether our
oppositional model can show that such norms are objectionable. It is
by citing facts opposed to those implied by the advertisement or
photograph, rather than simply by revealing its implicit ideological
code, that an ideological critique is made, for example by disputing
the typology of roles implied by advertisements directed at women.
What is essentially in dispute, is the unquestioned stereotype. This
can be seen if we look at Barthes's very well-founded attack on *The
Family of Man* photographic exhibition. He points out that its aim
was 'de montrer l'universalité des gestes humains dans la vie de tous
les pays du monde: naissance, mort, travail, savoir, jeux imposent
partout les mêmes conduites; il y a une famille de l'homme.'[8] The
family is thus 'moralized' and 'sentimentalized' into a 'mythe
ambigu de la "communauté humaine", dont l'alibi alimente toute
une partie de notre humanisme.'[9] However, as Barthes points out,
this humanism, which asserts that 'l'homme naît, travaille, rit et
meurt partout de la même façon' and that there is a 'human
essence', is revealed as merely sentimental if we pay attention
to other known facts which show on the contrary, 'différences'—
'que nous appelerons tout simplement ici des "injustices"'.[10] The
exhibition projects by its very unity of theme one picture, whereas
Barthes in opposition to this, would have preferred something quite
different which would show 'que l'enfant naisse bien ou mal, qu'il

coûte ou non de la souffrance à sa mère, qu'il soit frappé ou non de la mortalité, qu'il accède à telle ou telle forme d'avenir, voilà ce dont nos expositions devraient nous parler, et non d'une éternelle lyrique de la naissance.'[11] It is thus open to one of the general lines of objection in *Mythologies* as noted by Thody: 'the sign systems of modern society create a state of affairs which oversimplifies life's complex issues'.[12] It promotes the wrong type of consensus, as does of course all sentimental art, which tends to disregard the real nature of its object, as I. A. Richards pointed out long ago.[13]

The point thus turns, not on Barthes's unexceptionable and unsurprising analysis of the obvious theme of the exhibition, but on his ideological opposition to those themes. He dismisses the positive sentimental values of humanism, in favour of an attention to injustice, on the grounds presumably that the consolatory function of such an exhibition tends to make us forget or prevent us from becoming aware of the injustice. The grounds for opposition thus turn ultimately on the institutional power of the exhibition: an assessment of its likely success in its aims.

This institutional power is seen at its most disturbing in the case of television. Here the implications of the selection of topics for our attention and the narrative manner of their treatment are more serious. For we may rely on television for much of our knowledge of the world (seeing it as both mimetically transparent and institution-ally authoritative), and our ability to turn to alternative sources of information is the more limited, particularly in countries in which there is government control of television. We are less inclined to be aware of the ways in which it mediates reality, and may fail to see how its non-fictional modes (news, documentary, even games) are in fact literary in form and hence exploit quite artificial conventions.[14] These conventions may indeed be hidden from us by their very contemporaneity and emerge most clearly in historical perspective. We can all see how the Movietone News in the cinema of the 'thirties, 'forties, and 'fifties, for example, exploited a quite particular type of commentatory rhetoric. But the ideological aims of the interpreter, it is argued, should be to reveal such conventions in the present, and thus contribute, one imagines, to immediate political action or dissent.

We can see this in Fiske and Hartley's treatment of ITN's *News at Ten* which according to them illustrates Barthes's theory of myth.[15] In a programme on Northern Ireland on 7 January 1976 'the sign of the particular soldier becomes the *signifier* of the cultural values that he embodies in this news film. The "cultural meaning" of the soldier is what Barthes calls a *myth*', for example, that of 'ordinary men doing a professional and highly technological job . . . one of our

lads—professional—well-equipped (Private J. Smith)' (42). This is
'the myth of the British Army' reinforced by the sequence of scenes
and narrative handling in the bulletin. We look over his shoulder
(share his role of defending us) and accept the myth that soldiers are
'well-trained, special people', as propagated in Army recruiting
campaigns. This is reinforced by 'their' showing us the soldiers'
'ritualistic, crouching glide, in a predetermined order to predetermined positions' (43). An associated 'myth' of technological
expertise is reinforced by the photography of army equipment. Now
we should note that in this type of interpretation, factual description
or reporting is *defamiliarized* in the service of ideological criticism, by
the use of such terms as 'myth' and 'ritual'. Documentary, it is
implied, becomes fictional myth with its expected subordinate
component, a ritual. But the factual basis remains. The soldiers are
defending someone, if only themselves, they are well trained, they do
move in a certain way (how else could they be expected to behave in
a dangerous situation?) and do have a certain technological
expertise in using the equipment shown in the film. The implied sel-
ectivity and point of view of the film can be attacked only in so far as
it is fitted into an implied higher order set of myth-making
conventions, consonant for example with such authoritarian activities as the production of recruiting posters, and the attempt to make
an audience believe that the Army is professional and well equipped.
I do not in this wish to impugn the Fiske and Hartley interpretation;
only to reveal its underlying logic. Its essentially literary mode of
analysis is revealed if we see how they go on to treat the commentary
superimposed on such themes, as if it proceeded from an unreliable
narrator of a peculiarly biased kind.

    For they point out that this sequence concerning the Special Air
Service in Northern Ireland is introduced by the commentary
sentence, 'Mr Wilson is taking a carefully calculated risk' which
allows 'élite' individuals to be 'metonymically representative of
lesser mortals'. This reveals that 'the journalistic code takes account
of the primacy of individuals', so that 'what happened out there is
only a large-scale version of a generally available personal experience—a game of skill.' This is played on the board by tough
individuals (the SAS) who have a 'reputation earned behind enemy
lines' for toughness and resourcefulness like that in a war movie
(92). The higher order frameworks of the game and the movie genre
are supposed to account for the cultural salience of the codes within
the news, which subordinates fact to fictional modes. But it could of
course be the other way about. War movies of a certain kind (no
doubt exaggerated) get made because certain army groups do
indeed show these qualities even if doing so they act out those

mythological modes for behaviour which are part of their training. Once more the criticism implied here cannot impugn the truth of what we see. It suggests rather that the viewer is induced to place it within a conventionally reassuring fictional context. But the actual effectiveness of such procedures and their tendency to mislead is ultimately, as we have suggested earlier, a matter for empirical investigation.

A more overt ideological moral of the argument emerges in Fiske and Hartley's assertion that the British Army thus has a 'cultural function' not to win wars or kill people, but to 'withdraw from Britain's shrinking hegemony; to set a brave, well-trained face upon defeat'! (95). This is a 'contradiction', a part of the answer to their question 'how then are the contradictions *which we find in society at large* [italics mine] represented in the television media' (112). But the contradiction thus discerned depends upon the flat assertion by the interpreter of truths quite independent of any actually conveyed by the News: the assertions that Britain has a shrinking hegemony over Ireland, that it will be defeated in its attempt to maintain it, and that this reflects a contradiction in society. Any attempt to show the SAS in a positive light thus runs in the face of facts for which no independent evidence whatsoever is offered.

My aim in making these observations is not, needless to say, to defend any actions taken by the British Government, simply to show how the revelation of hidden ideology in a television programme depends upon a number of implied oppositional assertions that are never explicitly defended. But even if these implied political counter-assertions are discarded, we can still see that the analysis of a supposed documentary from a fictional point of view shows how the television programme can reflect, in its mass appeal, the general assumptions we (are urged to) make about the roles that society offers us to play (or, in another version, that the authorities make us play). I insert these more conspiratorial qualifications here because although Fiske and Hartley admit that there may be 'feedback' to those responsible for the News from 'people who watch', the system 'seems to operate with convenient advantages for the dominant section of society, whose preferred or sociocentral interpretations are most likely to be represented in the television message, and whose spokesman our bardic newsman might appear to be' (116).

However, the basic and I think the most telling accusation against the News of this kind (apart from the fact that it may be taken to represent a dominant interest) is once more the Barthesian one, of oversimplification and omission from the interpreter's point of view. Thus Seymour (an ITN newscaster) is criticized for his implication that terrorism in Northern Ireland is 'merely criminal', which fits

into a 'familiar individualist mythology' and thus fails to 'articulate . . . all the contradictory notions we may hold about Northern
Ireland' in his bulletin (113 f.) This is surely a tall order. The story
he tells can be understood easily, but 'whether or not it is accepted
as an appropriate way of understanding the complexities of
Northern Ireland politics is another matter, which will be decided
by a much larger and more diffuse cultural process, a kind of
collective bargaining whereby dominant definitions of the situation
are negotiated and established' (116). What is actually being asked
for once more, under a hierarchizing and politically tendentious
notion of 'collective bargaining', is liberal debate.

The interpretations we have been reporting make an ideological
extension of the Barthesian critique of realism we have earlier
discussed. Thus Fiske and Hartley typically argue that 'realism' as a
'characteristically bourgeois mode of representation' denies us
'access to alternative ways of seeing' and thus produces a 'con-
sumerist, non-critical attitude in the audience' (162 f.).

They thus extend the hermeneutics of suspicion, and the
oppositional model of interpretation. This is not to say that they do
not also reveal the epistemological unreliability, through literary
convention, of many of our codes of communication. But this
unreliability does not simply come from within (the programme may
be defended as factually truthful after all) but by displacing its
original institutional context. The News is seen generically, as part
of a system of conveying impartial information about the world, but
where the information is the focus of concern and dispute, the
programme may be seen to slant its treatment, and in doing so, by
offering so to speak a single channel of information, it fails,
according to its ideological critics, to do justice to the facts that *they*
consider important. Its subject-matter is really appropriate to
another genre altogether, that of criticism and debate. But the best
way of resisting the dominant ideology in all the examples so far
cited is, not surprisingly, to bring its existence out into the open and
to discuss it. But any liberal committed to the position that differing
views should be allowed to compete will agree with this, and with
the implication of these critics that the dominance of media
information can lead to unfair competition in a society in which
political views show considerable divergence.

The key to the Marxist character of this type of critique lies in its
appeal to the concept of class. But if the dominant ideology and its
preferred literary modes of expression are 'bourgeois' in origin, what
should be the origins, allegiances, and interests of its critics?
Ideological interpretation here tends to be made in the interests of a
particular group in society, whose voice is repressed or repressively

tolerated so long as it does not threaten a framework of apparently consensual belief whose dominance is disguised; as we shall see in the following section.

6.3 Marxism and the Dominant Ideology

> Certains veulent un texte (un art, une peinture) sans ombre, coupé de l''idéologie dominante'; mais c'est vouloir un texte sans fécondité, sans productivité, un texte stérile (voyez le mythe de la Femme sans Ombre). Le texte a besoin de son ombre: cette ombre, c'est *un peu* d'idéologie, *un peu* de représentation, *un peu* de sujet: fantômes, poches, traînées, nuages nécessaires: la subversion doit produire son propre *clair-obscur*.
>
> (On dit couramment: 'idéologie dominante'. Cette expression est incongrue. Car l'idéologie, c'est quoi? C'est précisément l'idée *en tant qu'elle domine*: l'idéologie ne peut être que dominante.)[1]

Our treatment of hidden ideology thus far makes it seem like a framework of belief whose shortcomings are to be revealed by an interpretative criticism which takes a superior mimetic attitude to the visual image, work, programme, or text. It shows in effect that the 'responsibility for the object laid bare' to which Sartre alluded is not, in a larger philosophical or political context, all that responsible. Whereas the interpreter is, or purports to be so.

In more overtly Marxist criticism however, something more specific is meant by dominant ideology. (I am aware that there are many different kinds of Marxists. All I can claim here is that many of them deploy logical forms of argument like those outlined below. The methods of interpretation I discuss seem typical within current Marxist criticism.) The basic assertion here is, I think, that in our present historical context this ideology will always have certain 'bourgeois' features. We have seen this in our discussion of Barthes and had a hint of it in the assertion that realistic documentary is a characteristically bourgeois mode of representation on television. For according to Marx, class societies develop beliefs that reflect the material interests of the dominant class; and his twentieth-century successors feel that their media will broadcast them.

The historical argument on which this judgement depends is roughly as follows.[2] The dominant or at least rising ideology was once, in the period of the Enlightenment, progressive. It proclaimed equality, and opposed feudalism, the power of the Church, and the absolutism of rulers. Against these the power of reason itself could be seen to be revolutionary. Reason in power could claim the self-evident values of liberty, equality, and fraternity. Emancipation would be universal, humanist, in a world which was after all, full of individual human beings with a power of reason to which all could appeal. However, there came the Fall, implicit in both Romanticism[3] and the failures of 1848. The bourgeoisie in power simply refused to apply the ideals of personal emancipation from which they had profited, and the liberty it promised, to the mob or the proletariat, nor have they since.[4] The history here is of course extremely crude, and could be disputed or refined *ad infinitum*, but that is hardly the point. All ideologues carry some such picture in their heads, and it is not difficult to assent in any case to its general outline.

According to the Marxist, it is in this refusal of a liberating alliance with the proletariat that lies the deep impoverishment of the bourgeois world-view, along with the paradoxical claim by the bourgeoisie, that their world-view is in fact *universal*.[5] This hubristic universalist claim guarantees that the bourgeois consciousness is in fact a false consciousness, whose inherent self-contradictions, particularly concerning liberty, become more and more apparent as the bourgeoisie in power fails to live up to those enlightenment ideas which gave it birth.[6]

This 'false consciousness' is a form of self-interest on the part of a group, its conscious or unconscious willingness to disregard the claims, for example to equality of power, made by another group. Lukács thus argues for an interesting case:

a political order suitable for the maximum development of the capitalist mode of production was created in the English Civil Wars by members of the incipient bourgeoisie in the course of pursuing various religious fantasies. The more the members of the bourgeoisie know about the nature of capitalist society, the less effective they will be in the class struggle because the more hopeless they will realise their situation to be in the long run. So the bourgeoisie, paradoxically enough, has an interest in being self-deceived.[7]

(This was a conclusion Swift also came to, for rather different reasons.) This attempt to avert one's gaze from disagreeable facts will not always be completely successful. One will, so to speak, knock up against them, and then try to retreat in a dishonest direction as Dickens seems to do in his treatment of trade unions in *Hard Times*. Our analysis of Barthes on *The Family of Man* also shows some of this process in action. The Marxist critic will go further than this and maintain that tensions within the capitalist system will inevitably reveal themselves under interpretation, even in those cases in which the bourgeois world-view is most confidently asserted.

There are thus two possible tasks for interpretation from this point of view. Firstly to show how, directly or indirectly, the work expresses the dominant ideology.[8] Secondly to show how this leads the text into contradictions which are symptoms of its false consciousness, which it will always attempt to suppress, but which interpretation can reveal. In interpretation the first task is implicitly performed in carrying out the second.

We can see one way in which these two forms of argument might combine in Lukács's discussion of Balzac, a reactionary writer who was yet to be praised for revealing the 'real' issues at stake, the inner tensions of capitalist society.[9] Similarly, Thomas Mann is analysed as a writer whose theme of the artist and his turn to aestheticism, which is a sympton of the decay of humanism, showed an acute consciousness of the historical crisis and dilemma of the German bourgeoisie. And yet, according to Slaughter, 'Lukács fails to carry through to the end this criticism of Mann, because he will not consider the implications of the revolutionary role of the German working class against the bourgeoisie.'[10] The gaze is averted.

The text may thus be taken not in terms of the writer's conscious world-view, but in terms of his implicit grasp of those gaps and splits in it that might lead to the revealing of an alternative one. It is this attempt to reveal hidden implications of the text consistent with their ideology that is crucial to much Marxist interpretation.

For Tolstoy can be read as expressing the world-view not simply of the aristocrats and landed proprietors he seems to be concerned with, but also of a more progressively revolutionary class, the Russian peasantry. As Bennett argues, he thus points to 'the class struggle as "already known" in the terms of Marxist theory'.[11] Tolstoy can be shown to have been aware of the 'essential contradiction' within his historical period.

What Lukács is looking for is the ability of the novelist, in this case Tolstoy, to develop fictional themes which can be related to their historical and social foundation. This is a task which Maupassant signally fails to perform in *Une Vie*, by isolating psychological from social problems.[12] 'For Maupassant society was no longer a complex of vital and contradictory relationships between human beings, but only a lifeless setting.'[13] Lukács is looking in his criticism on the other hand for the 'real relationships' of characters and the social motives of which they might be unaware. Thus Tolstoy comes 'very close' to 'the western realities' partly because of his growing aversion to the Russian ruling classes:[14] 'when Anna Karenina breaks through the limits of the common-place she merely brings to the surface in tragically clear intensification the contradictions blatantly present (although their edges may be blurred) in every bourgeois love and marriage'.[15] Lukács wonders how Tolstoy could do this even though he did not understand the socialist movement. The answer is largely because he was 'the poet of the peasant revolt' of 1861–1905. His treatment of this on an ethical basis is frequently 'incorrect and reactionary';[16] nevertheless he puts the right questions, and his characters' predicaments are related, by Lukács at least, to larger political events: 'the spiritual crises of Bezukhov and Bolkonski are reflections of the great current which broadened politically into the Decembrist rising' and in *Anna Karenina* one can 'feel the undertow of capitalism' in Oblonski's corruption by the officialdom which will help him to supplement his income from estates.[17] It is Tolstoy's epic grasp of the 'totality of objects' in his novels that makes him capable of grasping these tensions, though Lukács here argues for a very Dickensian complicity of the object to capitalism. Thus in 'The Death of Ivan Ilyich', 'the fading world of court sittings, card parties, visits to the theatre, ugly furniture, down to the nauseating filth of the dying man's bodily functions, is here integrated to a most vivid and animated world in which each object eloquently and poetically expresses the soul-destroying emptiness and futility of human life in a capitalist society'.[18]

But the real source of Tolstoy's genius lies in his embracing the viewpoint of the exploited peasantry in a way that is coincident to that of Lukács. This may seem eccentric, as though we are expected to view Romeo and Juliet from the point of view of Friar Lawrence. But Tolstoy was always, according to Lukács, capable of grasping the inter-relation between the classes, asking of each character 'in what way was their life based on the receipt of ground rents and on the exploitation of the peasants and what problems did this social basis produce in their lives?'[19] This is shown for example in the conversations of Levin with his brother and later Oblonski concerning the justification of private property. Of course Lukács's thesis that Tolstoy wrote from the peasant's point of view cannot literally be sustained: his 'philosophy' is actually entirely 'false'. And so he has none of that theoretical insight into the nature of capitalism or 'the revolutionary movement of the working class' which the Marxist would claim to possess,[20] but he does concern himself it seems with at least those facts which can support a Marxist analysis which is independent of his text, for 'nevertheless he gave us admirably lifelike and true pictures of Russian society'.[21] What he could not know was his own position in history: as Lenin pointed out, Tolstoy's views 'expressed the contradictory conditions of Russian life in the last third of the nineteenth century' but he makes nevertheless a 'protest against approaching capitalism, against the ruination of the masses and their divorcement from the land, which had to arise from the patriarchal Russian countryside.' He 'is great as the expression of the idea and sentiments that took shape among the millions of Russian peasants at the time the bourgeois revolution was approaching in Russia'.[22]

The interpretative strategies we have so far discussed thus attempt to adjudicate a particular type of relationship between the text, the historical reality it represents, and the later written history of its context. As we have seen, this is a typical function of interpretation. It is justified if at all on pragmatic grounds, as the mode of interpretation subserves the ideology. What is distinctive about the Marxist approach is that it claims to have a true interpretation of the process of contextual history in advance, and hence to be able to judge the degree of fit of the work or its interpretation to that paradigm, as Bennett's remark cited above, about 'the class struggle as already known', reveals. We are, as Jameson puts it, all part of a 'vast unfinished plot' of class struggle as diagnosed by Marx and Engels in *The Communist Manifesto*, so that through the text we may see the 'repressed and deeply buried reality of this fundamental history'.[23]

As things are, with few explicitly Marxist literary works in sight, this type of interpretation inevitably falls into the model of opposition. It has a standard whereby it can judge works to be reactionary or progressive as it expresses world-views which are or are not in accord with this 'plot'. It can only avoid predictability by showing an ability to discover and reveal the hidden ideological implications of texts, rather than by making a simple match of the work to its own world-view, which many Marxists claim to be 'scientific' and to that degree of a superior certainty: 'Historical materialism stands or falls by the claim that it is not only not an ideology, but that it contains a scientific theory of the genesis, structure, and decline of ideologies.'[24] As we have already seen, it is the deconstructive approach to the text which is most attuned to the detection of such hidden contradictions, and it is not surprising that the most subtle of recent Marxist criticism has been influenced in this direction. It is the deconstructive interpretation of the text, a revelation of its hidden aporias, that might prove most useful to an interpreter who is looking for elements within it which are in conflict with its own apparently dominant bourgeois ideology.

Pierre Macherey was the pioneer of this type of interpretation. One of his most significant arguments is that our usual treatment of the literary work as unified and coherent is an unnecessary idealization: 'du point de vue de l'analyse théorique, l'œuvre se dispose comme un centre d'intérêt; mais cela ne signifie pas qu'elle soit elle-même centrée'.[25] Derridan self-contradiction is brought up to the level of ideology, of which it was always capable. We can thus search for the 'non-dit' of the work, which is not simply a lack to be filled in by the reader, but an internal conflict of meaning, 'le conflit de plusieurs sens' which is not 'resolu, absorbé par le livre, mais par lui seulement montré'[26] and it is only the act of interpretation which can reveal the nature of this lack, of what fails to get said. Macherey's approach is very close, as he himself points out, to psychoanalytical interpretation, where the manifest content may overlie an internal latent tension which the text seeks to deny. And this gives rise to 'l'inconscient de l'œuvre (non de son auteur) . . . ce qu'on cherche est analogue à ce rapport que Marx admet quand il demande de voir derrière tout phénomène idéologique des rapports matériels relevant de l'infrastructure des sociétés . . . d'où la possibilité de *ramener* l'idéologique à l'économique.'[27]

Just as the analyst has a superior theory of the psychological mechanisms underlying the use of language, particularly when it reports the imagined or fantasized, the Marxist has a superior theory of political conflicts inherent in the historical period in and of which the writer writes, and of which the writer, not usually a Marxist, is not *ipso facto* aware. It confers upon the text a particular social context of utterance which reveals a particular unintended meaning, one often enough calling for a symbolic interpretation of the text which, as we saw in the case of *La Peste*, has to rise to a political statement at the level of allegory. We can see how this is if we look at Macherey's interpretation of Verne.

He points out that the overt exploration themes of Verne's works reflect the aspirations of the bourgeoisie concerning the conquest of nature and of the French colonial empire by industry. Common to both are the central themes of Verne's work: 'le voyage—l'invention scientifique, la colonisation'.[28] The last of these is the least apparent or less often 'mis en valeur, comme si on avait voulu le dissimuler ('given any value, as if with the intention of disguising it') because the typical scientist or engineer or rich man who is Verne's hero will conquer, annex, or displace the known towards the unknown, and thus use his power as a means of appropriation. This theme emerges most essentially for Macherey in Verne's *L'Île mystérieuse* (1875) which is a variation, so he says, on Robinson Crusoe and its theme of origin (227). For an island is a place in which the ideological elements of nature, industry, science, society, work, and so on can be 'ordered' from the beginning, as in colonization. In this case we have an island which is unrealistically well endowed with natural resources (228, 231, 240). But Verne's novel differs from Defoe's in a more important respect, because it starts off not with a single hero who has to establish his society but with a group of people who wish to transform their island into a new America (243), by establishing everything on the island from a primitive factory to electricity, including a telegraph which puts them in contact with a mysterious Captain Nemo. This mysterious contact breaks the main line of the story and its ideological realization, by imposing upon the reader an intrigue which seems to him 'more real'. For the island seems not to be in the state of 'une nature neuve' but artificial; a place for experiment, inhabited by 'une force inconnue' (243), which provides the castaways with a chest of goods. This contradicts any notion of simple conquest, for the island no longer seems to belong to the group. They are being acted upon rather than acting; as it turns out, by Nemo, who is hidden in the depths of a volcano and is the secret artist of the décor which surrounds them. When Nemo dies, the island disappears. Nemo is thus 'un autre savoir' or perhaps even a form of providence or God (248, 250). In any case he contradicts the myth of progress which is implied in colonization, and the book is thus not about possession but about the dispossession of colonizing work by fiction, for Nemo is a fantastic fictional figure. According to Catherine Belsey, he thus behaves rather like a subconscious impulse, as 'an unpredicted and contradictory element, disrupting the colonialist ideology which informs the conscious product of the work . . . his influence on the fate of the castaways from a subterranean cave, is the source of the series of enigmas and the final disclosure which constitutes the narrative. But his existence in the text has no part in the overt ideological project.'[29] And in the even more explicitly allegorical terms of Bennett, he is taken to show that 'nature's extremities . . . prove always to be already occupied, just as did the countries which were on the receiving end of France's colonising mission.'[30] This brings the problem of native populations to notice indirectly, subverts the Robinson Crusoe myth of pure origin which had been interpreted to show that economic organization could start from nothing, and shows how the colonizing ideology could or should be contested. It also shows the confusion of the bourgeois notion of rapport between science and nature. We are thus encouraged to read the book by Macherey and his followers 'a rebours de ce qu'elle voudrait dire' ('in a sense opposite to that which it intends') (255) and as reflecting 'contradictions réelles' (258), so that the moral of it all is that the bourgeois can never be alone, can never conquer the absolute, can never discover virgin nature, and can only be the master of a certain number of social relations (263). In this way Verne reveals 'the limits' of the 'coherence' of his ideology. And as we know from Derrida it is at the limits that ideologies break down. This will emerge if we wish not to show how a work is unified, but to reveal the nature of its omissions, to which it points, but which it does not describe: 'in its absences and in the collisions between its divergent meanings, the text implicitly criticizes its own ideology.'[31] What the text fails to say the interpreter will obligingly provide.

This type of interpretation thus runs counter to that practice within Anglo-American criticism which aims to show the unity and coherence of the work, and thus assumed even in difficult cases such as *The Waste Land* or the *Cantos* that inconsistencies and ambiguities, allusions and connotations, could all be subdued to a coherent thematics. This deconstructive approach can be directed to a further end. It not only attempts to reveal ideologically significant inconsistencies in the text, but attempts to show the superiority of this type of interpretation over others which refuse to consider such political implications. This contest has two aspects. First, its attack on an alternative 'humanist' or moralizing type of interpretation, and secondly, its assumption that the superior insight into history and politics guaranteed by Marxism can override such alternatives. This can be seen I think in the historically very scrupulous interpretation of *Adam Bede* by Widdowson and others.[32] Their aim is to combat an orthodox Leavisite approach to the text, with its 'reactionary' appeal to 'standards' or the 'civilized values' of the 'university', with its corresponding belief in 'an autonomy of the human spirit for which economic determinist and reductive interpretations of the class war left no room', and its 'ideological appropriation of the literary text' to subserve a nostalgia for that rural 'organic community' which was a central theme in Leavis's criticism (4).

Ideology appears in the text in an Althusserian manner: the work of art has an 'internal distance' from the ideology it is 'bathed' in, and ideology itself is pejoratively defined as 'the imaginary relationship of individuals to their real conditions of existence' (5). These real conditions of course exist *outside* the text in the interpreter's version of the nineteenth century, but they are alluded to inside it, and so the interpreter will wish to show that there is a 'dialectic between text and context, between 'realism' as a literary practice, and the real social relations which the realism at once both suppresses, or explains away, and implies in its solid specificity' (6 f.). Thus the author's sense of history and that of the interpreter will be put into competition. The text suggests a context or historical situation which the interpreter specifies. But the success of the enterprise depends very largely on the convincingness with which the interpreter can persuade us that the text does evoke such contexts. Thus although it is conceded that *Adam Bede* 'contains for the most part a coherent positivist–humanist explanation of the actions and the relations it proposes' it is also asserted, in pursuing a line of argument familiar to us from Macherey, that because of the 'partiality' of its 'world-view', 'tensions, irresolutions, absences, creases in the text will reveal themselves' (7). More properly, they will be revealed by the interpreter, for as we have seen the text cannot speak of its own implications. These tensions and so on appear in a context which it designs to be historically truthful. For George Eliot is at pains in her novel to tell us that she is a 'witness' on oath to the mirror of her mind as it recognizes the need (as ours should in following her) for sympathizing with and tolerating people as they are; so that for her 'Realism . . . is a way of making people understand and so sympathise with, their fellow men; it is the practice and form of humanism' (9). It claims faithfulness, completeness, and historical accuracy, and to these ends the portraits of the characters in the novel show how a configuration of character might reveal an underlying moral pattern. As this is worked out we may feel that *Adam Bede* 'is a strangely confident affirmation of bourgeois humanist ideology. By the end of the novel, the elements of egoism have been eradicated, Adam Bede has learnt sympathy through suffering, and has at the same time prospered, while Arthur Donnithorne of the landed gentry has not' (13).

Thus, they say, Arnold's Hellenistic humanism triumphs over the Hebraism of Methodism, in a world in which everything can be known rightly. All this will carry conviction 'so long as that [humanist] ideology remains the domain within which it is read and understood' (14)—but this is of course not good enough for Widdowson and his colleagues. What we see now is the oppositional model coming into view, in order to reveal the hidden contradictions of *Adam Bede*. One of the instances in which 'the realism slips' is Hetty's reprieve. Why should not Hetty be hanged? Why should she be transported, but die on her way back to England? The answer is that she cannot be thought of as becoming a prostitute. Even more revealingly, why is the method by which Arthur gets his reprieve not described? The answers are, because Hetty has fulfilled her place in the moral schema and must be removed 'hors de combat', and because the barbarity of hanging cannot be assimilated to the humanitarian perspectives of the novel. (One might ask, why not?) Nor could any explanation of Arthur's use of privilege in obtaining Hetty's reprieve find a place in the novel because 'it would introduce a dimension of public affairs (especially class influence) inimical to the world view George Eliot is propagating—let alone being a digression from the focus of the novel' (14). Similarly excluded is any notion of Methodism as a powerful social movement, which was successful in towns in this period, since all we hear of it is through Dinah in the rural context of Hayslope. Thus George Eliot is implicitly blamed for excluding 'urban industrial communities' from her novel. And yet 'Dinah's presence . . . invokes the absent contexts' as she 'creates around her extra textual space' (16). This theme of the absent context of Methodism is developed in a historical sketch of some length (21 ff.) from its early appeal at the time of the novel's narrative to the working class, to its growth into respectability amongst the middle classes at the time of its publication.

It is when we turn to these external historical contexts, rival evidence so to speak, that *Adam Bede*'s shortcomings can be seen. For the 'hints or suppressions or silences' which turn us towards them reveal a 'latent structure' which limits the explicit ideology of the work, for this latent structure is informed by '*real social relations* in respect of work and class power' (29). These emerge most explicitly in the gap in social class which makes it impossible for Arthur to marry Hetty. It is difficult once more to set a limit to this argument, for surely all works will imply something about 'work and class power' which will be open to a Marxist interpretation? However it seems that we can discriminate between works in terms of their *value* on these grounds, for those works which most encourage this 'dialectic' are the better for it (thus *Adam Bede* is better than Mrs Oliphant's *Salem Chapel*, with which it is compared in this study). *Adam Bede* can thus reveal 'issues in mid-Victorian social relations, particularly concerning labour, class and the position of women which are potentially subversive' (37).

It is thus the productive *use* of the text within a reading or interpretation that ultimately counts. The political and moral position of the reader is put at stake. We may of course be sceptical (with the deconstructive arguments of Chapter 5 in mind) of the narrative or mythical quality that any purported account of the 'real relations' within society must possess. But we can see how the acceptance of such a narrative or historical analysis can place restrictions on the norms against which any text may be matched. The interpretative act of matching, the way in which it 'produces' a reading, is justified by its effect on the reader.

The issues raised by *Adam Bede* according to Widdowson and his colleagues, are thus subversive of the liberal humanism of George Eliot, and of the interpreter who would endorse it, once the series of perspectives between the co-text and its context have been opened up. For once we are aware of these relationships, 'we will confer "value" not simply on those works which most nearly achieve a formal coherence or those which are more transparently ideological, but on those whose cognisance is such that it opens the dialectic between the internal world a work presents and the historically precise "real relations" in which it stands' (38).

The force of this type of interpretation thus lies in its insistence on the similarity or dissimilarity between the world of the co-text and the historical context of its production, and the urging of independent grounds for considering these important. The focus of the text is changed; in this particular type of case, from the individual's conscious concerns to the context of the 'real social relations' in which he or she is found. This strategy is supposed to reveal a hidden and essentially unadmitted, potentially subversive, 'political unconscious' for the text. The interpreters' behaviour is in respects like that of a psychoanalyst; his notion of real relationships (of the dynamics of the family, for example) is apparently correct, and it is only a repression due to self-deception or a 'false consciousness' promoted by self-interest that can prevent the reader from admitting its truth. If the Marxist really possesses a superior insight into the relationship of psyche and history, any resistance to this insight (such as a preference for 'moral' language) is evidence of the repression or 'mystification' inherent in the realist mode of the text we have discussed. Any shift to 'liberal humanist' or moralist premisses divorced from political analysis is a sympton of evasion, and will supposedly reveal further self-contradiction.

There are of course a number of objections to the logic of this type of argument, which is crucially dependent upon the truth of its superior theory of historically conditioned relationships. It is in fact of considerable generality : since it points to implications for texts of which their authors (and original audiences) could not possibly have been aware. It involves an historical recontextualization of the text : like looking for the origins of the New Testament in the Old, or as Ian Watt has shown with respect to *Robinson Crusoe*, for the outline of Tawney's thesis concerning religion and the rise of capitalism in Defoe,[33] or like recapitulating the life-history of Hamlet in terms of Freudian theory. The Marxist character of the interpretations we have discussed only really emerges in the assumption that such unrecognized meanings will be in contradiction to the dominant or bourgeois or ruling-class ideology. And obviously enough the Marxist view of the development of capitalism, of class conflict, and so on, will conflict with the overt ideology of the nineteenth-century liberal text. But I wish in what follows to look a little more closely at the contention that Marxist recontextualizing interpretations of this kind may conflict with or supersede liberal or 'humanist' moral interpretation.

6.4 The Moral and the Political

The basic line of attack here is on the universality and immutability of moral concepts, and the anchoring of them in individuals. Thus Jameson argues that 'ethical thought projects as permanent features of human "experience" and thus as a kind of "wisdom" about personal life and inter-personal relations, what are in reality the historical and institutional specifics of a determinate type of group solidarity for class cohesion.'[1] And Eagleton believes that once an analysis on these lines is given, we can abolish 'morality' as an 'autonomous discourse': 'The notion that there is a privileged "moral level" at which the object is to be evaluated disappears: the moral becomes coterminous with the political.'[2]

Individualist moral concepts are thus seen as entrenched in historical circumstances in a way which the humanist will deny, and the Marxist demonstrate. We may doubt the universality of moral judgements (or of associated literary doctrines such as that of the 'eternal human heart') once we realize that complexes of moral beliefs change through time (or at least relative to one another) and so may be taken to express in historical context the power relations and the typologies of character that subserve them. Shakespeare has a particular view of the virtues of a king; George Eliot seems to emphasize the 'feminine' moral virtues of compassion, tolerance, and resignation, which confirm the subordinate role of women; and we may think the Sicilian's act of revenge wrong whereas his community thinks it right. Indeed, the moral views of a social community like that of the English in India as represented by E. M. Forster or Paul Scott, may seem as restricted and defensive of power relations as those of the Sicilians. However novels such as those I have just alluded to also seem to concentrate upon a 'liberal' independent and individualist moral judgement, which seems to arise from a hostility to the use of moral judgement to strengthen class cohesion.

The Marxist view may thus far be universally true, but trivially so. By this I mean that all moral codes will reflect more or less temporary consensual agreements amongst individuals who have a more or less homogeneous social standing, and who accept that moral discourse will be bound up with the authority or power of individuals or groups, if only to make praise or blame effective. However, although there may be interesting cases of the abuse of group solidarity, as shown by Forster and other novelists, particularly in the dystopian tradition, which runs from Zamyatin's *We* through Huxley's *Brave New World* and Orwell's *Animal Farm* and *1984* to Anthony Burgess's *A Clockwork Orange* and *1985*, these very examples show how the group is vulnerable to the dissenting judgement of any individual who takes this very fact about the use of the moral code he is expected to embrace into account. There may thus be a 'second order' degree of responsibility for our moral and political beliefs which resides within the individual (even though the pathos of the books above is to show how such individual dissent may be mastered by authority).

It is this notion of autonomous responsibility, threatened though it may be by social forces, which has been central to recent moral philosophy, and to the tradition of moral interpretation of literature. 'Moral interpretation' may of course be diversely understood; we may approve of works because the codes we discern in them appear to coincide with our own, or wish to censor them because they do not. But in what follows I wish to treat moral interpretation as it arises from and is defended by moral philosophy : that is, as concentrating upon the principles of action and the reasons for defending them given by individuals; and hence upon the interaction of belief and intention, emotion and will. This conceptual framework may lead the critic to treat the text as raising the problems of free will and moral responsibility.[3]

Indeed, moral philosophers in the Anglo-American and existentialist traditions have tended to define their concerns as centred upon the individual. William Frankena argues quite typically, that although morality may be a 'social enterprise' which exists before the individual and thus is 'social in its origins', ethical concerns can only arise when 'we can think for ourselves' and achieve 'autonomy as moral agents'. The rules of society are thus 'so internalised that we can be said to be inner-directed, to the stage in which we think of ourselves in critical and general terms.'[4] We become autonomous beings who may refuse 'other-direction' by society, for distinctively moral reasons.[5]

The work of moral philosophers thus tends to derive from the Kantian assertion that the basis of the moral law is to be found in the subject as capable of autonomous will, and concentrates on the moral thinking of the individual as isolated, rational and capable of asking what is right or ought to be done.[6] (I should perhaps add here that such thinkers do not seem yet to have addressed themselves to the conflict between the social and the individual that I am about to discuss; and that what follows will have to be regarded as very speculative. Much more rigorous work needs to be done.[7])

A few quotations from a 'casebook' on Scott Fitzgerald's *Tender is the Night* may help us to appreciate in more detail how the features of moral thinking outlined above operate in interpretation.[8] The critics concentrate a good deal on the book's hero, Dick Diver. He has 'good instincts' which are related to the virtues operative in his society—those of the American South: 'honour, courtesy and courage' (9). But his more private 'hidden weakness' is a 'respect for money' and a great need to be admired (10). This leads to his decline, as Fitzgerald himself pointed out. He capitulates to the values of the expatriate society which surrounds him despite the responsibilities of his social role and the valuable abilities associated with it: 'The novel should do this. Show a man who is a natural idealist, a spoiled priest, giving in for various causes to the idea of the haute bourgeoisie, and in his rise to the top of the social world, losing his idealism, his talent and turning to drink and dissipation' (14).

It is Dick's inability to sustain the moral rather than the clinical responsibilities of this role, that leads to his decline':

Diver . . . is sapped of his strength because he is forced to become the father figure, first to Nicole Warren . . . then to Rosemary Hoyt, Hollywood star and 'Daddy's Girl', and finally to the whole group of immature inebriated Americans that frequent the Riviera after the First World War . . . As a device for indicating both the decadence and the infantilism of the thirties this is highly successful. (54).

His decline under these pressures is nevertheless seen in pretty unforgiving moral terms by his critics: he 'fails to work' (55), is the victim of his vanity (67), 'commits symbolic incest' with Rosemary Hoyt (68), 'there is no mature commitment in him' (68), and he has 'the defect of uncontrollable generosity' (110). This amounts to a rather heavy-handed moral condemnation, though some interpreters, for example William Troy, see the book as posing for the reader the problem of deciding how far Dick is responsible for his acts: 'We are never certain whether Diver's predicament is the result of his own weak judgement or of the behaviour of his neurotic wife. At the end we are strangely unmoved by his downfall because it has been less a tragedy of will than of circumstance' (127).

The critics, like Fitzgerald, see Dick's vices and virtues and weak judgement as intimately related to his social role and indeed his representative status; one critic remarks that Dick Diver possesses 'the intellectual legacy available at Johns Hopkins, Oxford, and Vienna. If that mind can crack . . . all men of mind should take notice' (x). And yet it is his inner psychological reactions that are the main focus of attention. William Troy alone suggests that the society in which he lives may be the controlling 'circumstance' of his story; but in terms of the moral philosophy we have so far indicated, the critics' analysis only makes sense on the assumption that moral decisions may take place in some inner free forum of the mind. This is an assumption which is explicitly defended within the liberal tradition of interpretation of character familiar to us in the work of Leavis, Steiner, Bayley, Swinden, Langbaum, and others.[9] Thus W. J. Harvey in *Character and the Novel* argues that the novel in the nineteenth and twentieth centuries, with its 'intrinsic' or internal presentation of character, encourages this notion of subjectivity of the self as the 'secret central ego lurking behind a gallery of social personae' and even as possessing 'a heart of darkness in the character, a central mystery which is never quite presented'.[10] Even when social conditions impinge on character, the novel, and especially the existentialist novel,[11] may convincingly present the free individual, deciding and choosing in the context of a future which within the fiction seems indeterminable. Indeed the tradition of the novel shows that diversity and individuality are thought of as valuable and as ends in themselves, partly because 'most human beings will always elude or overflow the categories of any ideology'.[12] It also encourages in the reader 'a clash between sympathy and detachment' and hence the virtues of tolerance, scepticism, and respect for the autonomy of others.[13]

It is this conception of the novel and its proper interpretation that is challenged by many Marxist critics, who wish to see the conflict between the individual and the social in an opposing and indeed opposite perspective. We can trace the beginnings of this alternative if we look at Terry Eagleton's analysis of *Middlemarch*.[14] He argues that we have here on the one hand a Romantic individualism (Feuerbachian humanism) concerned with 'the untrammeled evolution of the free spirit' and on the other 'the inevitable social laws to which Romantic individualism, if it is to avoid both ethical anarchy and social disruption, must conform' (111). It 'must' so conform, one assumes, because the individualist who thinks he is free must in the end recognize that he or she performs a social role which comes to define (often enough in George Eliot by a process of attrition) his or her identity. Thus Eagleton attributes ideologies or 'totalities' to each of the characters in the novel, who are fixed by him in a typology—Casaubon is an idealist, Lydgate a scientific rationalist, Bulstrode an evangelical Christian, Dorothea a romantic self-achiever—and 'each of these totalities crumbles, ensnared in the quotidian' (119). This view of the relationship of individual to ideology runs counter to that cited from Harvey.

However, Eagleton believes that ideological conflict is 'defused and repressed' by George Eliot, partly because it is seen to be too much rooted in a conception of rural society which oversimplifies 'the whole social function' (112) and also precisely because she sees the issues raised in her novels too exclusively in the terms of individual moral judgement, in which 'since every destiny is significant, each is consequently relativised' (114) by the distribution of the author's and reader's sympathy. This need to sympathize and compromise with individuals evades recognition of the ideological oppositions they represent. Indeed 'Eliot's fiction . . . displays from the outset a conflict between ideological totalities which outstrip classical liberalism, and a fear of the disruptive effect of such totalities on the "personal" values bred by that liberal lineage' (118). Even the desire for political reform in *Middlemarch* is evasively moralized, since 'the cautious empiricism of the bourgeois liberal tradition . . . is in itself an ideologically inadequate response to the moment of post-Reform Bill England, with its demand for a more intensely incorporating ideology' (119). The novel is thus inadequate to its epoch as Eagleton conceives it, because its world is 'transplanted' from the 'historical' to the 'ethical' (120). This is a 'mystification' which allows the moralizing interpretation to dominate; it is indeed 'inherent in the very form of realistic fiction, which by casting objective social relations into inter-personal terms, constantly holds open the possibility of reducing the one to the other' (121). This is an 'ethical reduction of history' (ibid.). The categories of interpretation are thus inverted; the individual is seen as subject to those larger historical forces whose political importance should earn them the focus of our attention.

The moves in argument that Eagleton makes here are crucial to our understanding of the locus of the conflict between 'liberal' and 'Marxist' interpretation. Sympathy with the individual as such, as the independent site of psychological and moral conflict, has to be given up, or at least modified. For in the larger (and, as Eagleton would argue, more comprehensive) context of political interpretation, the individual has to be seen as representative of forces within society which transcend him or her, and of which he may not even be wholly conscious. We would have to suspend those values implicit in our sympathy and respect for the sheer diversity of individuals, and resist the temptation to shut out the historical context (so far as we understand it) within which they operate. We would not for example allow our awareness of the historical evolution of class differences to collapse, via personal sympathy, into a merely 'moral' relationship which will relativize our view of individuals in society. For such short-term views may blind us to the larger historical forces controlling individuals which the Marxist wishes to move into the centre of his interpretation.

We are dealing here with two competing sets of norms for interpretation, both of which are equally intelligible, which are both in some conditions intertranslatable (by 'inversion') and which are both going concerns in their appeal to different interpretative groups: those who would 'agree' with George Eliot, and those who like Eagleton would accuse her of fear and evasion of the political conflicts inherent in her period. We saw that Widdowson and his colleagues concede that *Adam Bede* offers a 'coherent positivist humanist explanation of its action' and of course the same can be said for *Middlemarch*. We have different frameworks of description for the same representations of character—the one individualist and psychological, the other social and political.

If we feel impelled to chose between such conflicting norms for interpretation, we must, as we argued earlier, look at the separate justifications within the conversation of critics, for their use, in terms of the ends which they are taken to serve. Catherine Belsey takes just such a pragmatic view: 'instead of looking at *Daniel Deronda* for the confirmation of a banal morality, it is more productive to read it, for instance, as challenging the sexual power relations of society, in ways which have an identifiable bearing on our own.'.[15] We are thus urged to see as implicit in the text an oppositional ideology that reveals a type of contradiction familiar to us from our analysis of Macherey; a conflict between the Victorian notion of marriage and that of individual freedom or sexual equality. And so the interpreter may attack any society (like our own) which sustains such contradictions. In doing this we may have to discount many variations in historical circumstances, and, indeed, the moral perspective (surely, hardly 'banal') of George Eliot as narrator, since 'to read *Daniel Deronda* as a feminist text is not necessarily to take it in the terms the narrative voice proposes as its own'.[16] Eagleton's view of *Middlemarch* as concerned with conflicting ideologies, and Widdowson's of the 'absent contexts' of Methodism in *Adam Bede*, equally put them in opposition to the narrator's viewpoint. This is in accord with a critical premiss clearly formulated by Eagleton: 'Criticism is not a passage from text to reader: its task is not to redouble the text's self-understanding, to collude with its object in a conspiracy of eloquence. Its task is to show the text as it cannot know itself, to manifest the conditions of its making (inscribed in its very letter) about which it is necessarily silent'.[17]

Although such arguments make clear (legitimately in my view) the differing ends served by interpretation, they do little to resolve the conflict; indeed they simply urge a dismissive evasion of moral discourse. But the political argument may I think be designed to do more than this. Its force lies in reminding us of how uncertain we are of the *boundary* between the individual and the social. It may indeed attempt to deconstruct this opposition. For once we allow such a conflict of interpretation to arise, we can see that we may be led into ideological contradiction, as Barbara Johnson showed in her analysis of 'Billy Budd'. For just such 'frameworks of reference' were in dispute there : those concerned with Billy's acts as emerging from his (autonomous) character, and those concerned with the nature of his acts as considered in a socio-legal context, subject to the imperative arising from his duties in the socially defined role of 'commissioned fighter'. The legal process here secured the victory of the political over the moral order; and it could be said that Eagleton and others use the process of political interpretation to secure an analogous victory, also based upon a premiss concerning the ultimate sources of power.

But the room for doubt here may not simply arise from our need to choose a framework in which to place the narrative of human action. It may involve a more profound dispute about the nature of the subject of action himself, should what we take as individual moral responsibility be shown to be the result of systems operating *through* the individual.

Thus Raymond Williams asks the interesting question, whether the concept of 'psychology' is individual or social.[18] A similar question can be asked of the moral subject of action.[19] A real doubt arises here if we can be brought to see that the moral codes of individual conscience, when expressed in language, have like all other codes a social aspect, and thus presuppose social roles (like those of the Sicilian avenger, or Dick Diver as psychiatrist or substitute father). Coward and Ellis thus attack the liberal notion of individualism as inherently suspect : according to them the 'human' is a 'socially constituted process', and the notion of 'human essence' can be 'discarded by a materialist ideology'.[20] It is thus 'idealist' and 'bourgeois' to present society 'as consisting of 'free' individuals, whose social determination results from their pregiven essences like 'talented' 'efficient' 'lazy' 'profligate' etc.'[21] For such terms express social judgements which the individual inevitably internalizes, under the illusion that he uses them 'autonomously'. (The analysis here depends upon Lévi-Strauss's notion of man as constructed by the symbol system and not as its 'origin'.) Thus even the most idiosyncratic of Dick Diver's moral attributes may ultimately be subsumed under his real and symbolic social roles as *haut bourgeois*, psychiatrist, and 'priest'. If his tragedy is less one of will than of social circumstance, those circumstances will be historical ones, which prescribe both the types of role he may play *and* the way in which he thinks about them.

This attempted dissolution or 'decentring' of the individual subject of action has already attracted a considerable literature.[22] This has relied heavily on Derridan arguments that the subject is 'inscribed' in language or is a 'function' of it.[23] Lacanian psychoanalytic theory also seems to supplement this: in Lacanian terms contradictions arise within the subject from the unconscious, as it attempts to disrupt the symbolic order as imposed by the family, and, ultimately, society. There is thus a 'dialectical' relationship between individuals and the language in which their subjectivity is constructed, and divisions within the subject will emerge at moments of crisis or transition in the social formation.[24] As we are initiated into the (Saussurean) symbol system of society (indeed, into the Hallidayan 'social semiotic' indicated at the outset) we take up, it is urged, a 'subject role' and hence an ideological describable position within it.

Unfortunately arguments of this kind even if they are descriptively correct, are open to a number of simple objections which seem to allow the individualist whom we described earlier to escape, and liberal moral discourse to survive. For if we accept the 'decentring' argument and suppose that our discourses 'put us in position' willy-nilly, so that we are no more than the bearers of certain conceptual categories, neither knowing completely nor mastering the discourses which produce us, we might well *then* ask with Bernard Sharratt, 'if the subject doesn't *know*, who or what *does* 'know' *that* "the subject" *doesn't* know? Does the unconscious know? Or perhaps Marxism knows? But does Marxism know that it knows? Or perhaps Marxism knows that "it" knows? Or perhaps *it* knows that Marxism knows—or doesn't know? We've been in this hole before, a long time ago.'[25] For once the nature of the social discourses that supposedly structure us as men and women in the world and in the text, is pointed out, we can do one of two things : either take responsibility for using them (the fact that the semaphor language I use is wholly dictated to me does not absolve me from letting the plane crash, in which case the 'moral subject' re-emerges), or change our discourse by looking at it critically, which is of course just what the Marxist wishes us to do, as it allows him to claim that he also has a morality, based upon a higher order series of assumptions concerning the broader context of human action. His enterprise presupposes that even if we are trapped by the dominant ideology (or whatever) we may be made free of it. If the subject then moves into another, equally 'socially determined' discourse, then we do have the possibility of an infinite regress : but it would nevertheless still make sense to argue that we can make rational decisions on the margins between such discourses once we were aware of them. And that awareness may simply depend on our historic luck, the luck that preserves us from believing in Greek gods, or demons or witchcraft, or whatever. We are lucky enough at present to realize that discourses such as those of overt ideology which we described at the outset, or those which 'inscribe' the subject, and the liberating discourse of Marxism, which argues that we are all, and particularly the workers,[26] taught to think of ourselves in the wrong way, are all relative to one another, and indeed that one of them may be dominant; but *ipso facto* we have a clue to adjudication between them. This is precisely what we are attempting to do, in contrasting individualistic and social types of interpretation.

We may see more fully how such ideas may arise within the interpretation of the text, if we look at Frederic Jameson's discussion of Conrad's *Lord Jim*, since he also wishes to argue that 'the literary 'character' is no more substantive than the Lacanian ego and . . . is to be seen rather as an 'effect of system' than as a full representational identity in its own right.'[27] Thus the 'meaning' of the subject 'can be traced back to the system that generates it' (243). If the interpreter can do this he will 'dissolve the verisimilitude of the character Jim' and at the same time 'discredit and despatch into critical dilettantism the whole thematics of heroism and individual guilt and expiation about which we have already complained' (243), which is in any case part of the 'feudal ideology of honour' (217). This will involve the 'shattering' of the book in our 'refusal to take it on its own organizational terms' as a novel which is 'completely organized around the investigation of a single individual destiny, a single unique and yet more largely consequent socially significant experience' (243). This suggests that even if Jim's acts may have an individualistic moral meaning (that indeed made explicit in the text) they also have a consequential social significance which will of course emerge in the historical recontextualization provided by interpretation. The question that faces us is whether the further significance is to be separately notified simply on pragmatic grounds, or whether it really does dispose of the moral analysis (in the way that an over-arching theory may subsume apparently scattered empirical observations within a larger generalization).[28]

The novel is thus 'rewritten' and re-read in terms of a social typology in which we see Jim as refusing to identify with the 'deck chair captains' (244; cf. *LJ*, 16[29]), or to submerge his individualism in the collectivity of the pilgrims. (245, cf. 253). The social system surrounding him thus generates for him (or in Jameson's terms 'in him') a peculiarly ambiguous position, one which as his failure in

Patusan will show, he cannot sustain. For Jim can be seen there as the exemplar of a man whose 'place' is 'blocked out' for him by 'the union of activity and value, of the energies of Western capitalism and the organic immanence of the religion of precapitalist societies' (255). When he comes to Patusan as a 'Romantic colonialist'[30] the contrast between his values (and presumably those of Gentleman Brown) and those of the community he is supposed to protect, reinforces our feeling of the relativity of such values (and leads to disaster when Brown repudiates a moral contract which Jim makes with him as a man of 'common blood' and common experience, *LJ* 219). Jim's failure here can obviously enough be seen in some such political terms, or at least those of a conflict of cultures, even if we thereby discount the thematic importance of the 'superb egoism' (*LJ*, 300) that leads him to his 'excessively romantic' death, in which he celebrates his 'pitiless wedding with a shadowy ideal of conduct' (*LJ*, 313). But what of the earlier jump? Can it really be maintained that ethical considerations here are merely 'diversionary'?

For *Lord Jim* at this point indeed insists on 'the problematics of the individual act' (264), and if we are to appreciate the way in which Jameson refuses to collude with the text, we must pay some attention to the Harveyesque analysis he thereby dismisses.

Much of the first part of the book builds up to Jim's own avowal of his state of mind at the Patna disaster: 'I had jumped . . . it seems' (*LJ*, 88). This is the end of an elaborate sequence of premonitory moral judgements by Marlow : 'if his sort can go wrong like that' (36) 'a more than criminal weakness' (38), 'he was one of us' (38, also 64, 85, 171, 272). Jim faces the inquiry 'practically of his own free will' (57), and when he speaks of his 'mistake' and of his being 'not ready' (66) Marlow feels that his account is symptomatic of 'those struggles of an individual trying to save from the fire his idea of what his moral identity should be' (66). There is thus plenty of scope for the interpretative discussion of Jim's degree of responsibility for his act, of the kind we described, in which 'heroic aspirations' encounter 'weakness' and very possibly circumstances so overwhelming that it is only their consequences of public disgrace rather than of guilt, that count : for as Jim remarks 'That is what I had to live down. The story didn't matter' (104). (Significantly enough, after this remark is reported, the French lieutenant gives his account of the matter, 107 f. and esp. 114–15). All interpreters will similarly infer slightly different 'stories' of Jim's act (like the one I have sketched above) which will tend to turn on the relationship of psychology to circumstance and of moral principle to will power.

But for Jameson the dynamics of the individual act are of little consequence, since 'the social at once washes back across it, to transform it utterly' (264). It is at this point that he wishes to reveal the larger significance of Jim's jump: 'Conrad pretends to tell us the story of an individual's struggle with his own fear and courage; but he knows very well that the real issues are elsewhere, in the social example Jim cannot but set, and the demoralising effect of Jim's discovery of Sartrean freedom on the ideological myths that allow a governing class to function and to assert its unity and legitimacy' (264). This class is not, as Marlow might suggest, merely the 'confraternity of the sea'; it is 'the ruling class of the British Empire, the heroic bureaucracy of imperial capitalism which takes that lesser, but sometimes even more heroic, bureaucracy of the officers of the merchant fleet as a figure for itself' (265). The 'extreme situation' which Jim enters is thus 'the precondition for the revelation of the texture of ideology' (265).

But there is no explicit indication of any such political status for Jim in Conrad's text. Such generalizations as we do find, tend to describe Jim in that 'universalizable' moral language of the virtues that is under attack. Marlow says for example that

He stood there for all the parentage of his kind, for men and women by no means clever or amusing, but whose very existence is based on an honest faith, and upon the instinct of courage. I don't mean military courage, or civil courage or any special kind of courage. I mean just that inborn ability to look temptations straight in the face—a readiness unintellectual enough, goodness knows, but without pose—a power of resistance . . . (38)

Critics like Jameson and Eagleton attack this sort of assessment because, like the moral judgements we have already cited, it is to be seen not as asserting something that is independently valid, but as part of a collective moral philosophy which tries to draw Jim, Marlow, Marlow's audience, and the reader, into a group expressing a kind of solidarity with one another which is vitiated by the fact that it is the solidarity of a group with a disputable position in the world.[31] Thus Eagleton says of Conrad that 'his positive values, incarnate above all in the virile solidarity of the ship's crew, are the reactionary Carlylean imperatives of work, duty, fidelity and stoical submission—values which bind men spontaneously to the social whole'.[32] Furthermore, even if we are alert to the fact that Jim's 'kind' here are the bourgeois or ruling classes or those in 'spontaneous' alliance with them, and that the judgements they express arise amongst the mere exponents of a social system that is not critically examined in the way that we have urged that it can be, I think we find that because of the refusal to 'collude' with the text, the exemplary quality insisted on here depends (as it does in

Eagleton's analysis of *Middlemarch*) entirely upon the interpreter's mediating statements. *He* asserts that Marlow's virtues have a 'Carlylean' character, or that Jim sets a social example of a particular kind, and also, rather surprisingly to my mind, that the 'imperial bureaucracy' took officers of the merchant marine as 'figures' for itself. This use of example and figure (like Eagleton's 'totalising ideologies') allegorizes the text on the basis of historical assertions concerning the relationship of the individual to the group that occur to no one within it. (They also depend upon a typology, ultimately derived from Lukács.[33]) Indeed Jameson earlier gives a sympathetic account of the anagogical level of allegory, as expressing the collective meaning of history, and as reconciling the private and the public (30 ff.).

His interpretation of Jim's jump thus involves, as he explicitly acknowledges, a recontextualization of the incident as described in the book : such materials are indeed 'utterly metamorphosed' by the interpreter 'when they are wrenched from the realm and categories of the individual subject to the new perspectives of collective destiny' (269), and are, rather unsubtly, given implications as acts with symbolic significance for the status of the governing class. The justification for this arises from the premiss of Marxist critics that literature can only be properly understood in the larger framework of social reality, and from the desire to affirm an independent collective narrative within history, one to which Jim contributes whether he knows it or not.

Jameson suggests that such an interpretation is somehow *part* of the text, in his use of causal terms such as those of 'tracing back' from the text to a 'generating system' or in demonstrating the 'consequences' of an action, and thus 'restoring' a 'socially concrete subtext' for it, part of a 'subconscious' meaning which is there even if Conrad (and we) may have 'preferred not to see it' (269). But this is not really the case. For his interpretative statements, like those cited from Widdowson and Eagleton above, are performing an essentially didactic function in affirming a theory which is independent of, and supplementary to, the text, indeed refuses to 'collude' with it. The 'true' implications of the text thus revealed may strike the reader as at least as 'banal' as those moral speculations within it that they are intended to supplant. And yet they purport to let the reader in on the secret inner history of the text and its context, and even of the writer's own pretence to be telling us one story when he knows that he should be telling us another.

In fact, the pragmatic justifications of moral and Marxist interpretations are rather similar. The moralist looks for a more complex understanding of the predicament of those with a 'shadowy deal of conduct' in such a way as presumably to make the reader's sympathetic response to real individuals similarly more complex.[34] Jameson also seems to believe that Jim's story will help to 'demoralise' anyone who is inclined to believe in the 'myth' which grants legitimacy to a governing class. There seems to be a moral lurking here too : if an officer–member of that class turns out to be a coward, he lets down the side, and sows a very fruitful doubt as to the fitness of the bourgeoisie to remain in command, a doubt indeed which, it is suggested by Jameson, leads to the suicide of Brierly, one of Jim's judges, which he describes as a 'class abdication' (264).

This suggests that even if we were convinced of Marxist political ends, we would not necessarily wish to give up the language of moral appraisal for individuals. They would in any case be urged to perform ideal-regarding actions in the light of equality and justice (though Marx himself might not have thought so, since he regarded evolution towards an egalitarian state as inevitable). But with historical hindsight, the contemporary Marxist may not be inclined to accept that Marxism is a 'scientific' ideology whose laws of historical development are ineluctable, and so consider socialism as merely a morality which tends to facilitate good ends.[35] It is thus a peculiarly theological question, whether man may really become the Kantian 'subject of ethics' only after he has ceased to play a social role cast for him by an unjust system, or has ceased to be alienated.[36] The Marxist critic at present will still wish to interpret the text for particular moral ends—disapproval of the ruling class, sympathy with the oppressed, and so on. What is basically at issue from our point of view is his ability to translate those moral judgements we still make into a second order political significance, to rewrite them 'in the stronger language of a more fundamental interpretative code.'[37] What the Marxist adds to the language of moral appraisal in theorizing our reading of the text then, are higher order explanations : (1) of the way in which it may arise as an expression of group solidarity and be dictated to the individual by the social system; (2) of its relativity when considered alongside the moral languages of other historically separated groups; and finally (3), of the need to discriminate between such groups as more or less 'progressive' towards stated political ends. Marxist critics consider the moral language of the bourgeoisie defective in all these three respects, as we have seen; but it is not internally incoherent, and so can only be criticized from the point of view of some higher-order aim which transcends it. Such higher order aims for the Marxist are contained within the political ideology which helps him to theorize his reading. One consequence of this, in Jameson's case, is the attempt to deconstruct or reverse the order of priority he sees in liberal moral thinking. Thus liberalism is only a possible world-view if 'the political and ideological are merely secondary or 'public' adjuncts to the content of a real 'private' life, which alone is authentic or genuine. It is not possible for any world-view—whether conservative or radical and revolutionary—that takes politics seriously' (289). Of course this grossly exaggerates the liberal hostility to the relationship between morality and politics,—indeed it wholly disregards the liberal tradition from Mill to Rawls—but at the same time it reveals the Marxist desire for an interpretative explanation which overarches or transcends the individual and his private concerns. The force of the Marxist argument thus depends upon the acceptability of his higher-order generalizations. For example, his ability to show how individual acts do express a class position. (There are analogous problems in Freudian theory in showing, e.g. how my acts *do* express hostility to a parent and so on.)

It depends in fact upon the willingness of particular individuals to rewrite all the idiosyncratic or original acts of other individuals in more generalized terms. For even the arguments of Jameson and others have their own individual force (and form) as an expression of their views. Any expression of class solidarity can only be made by an individual, and the acceptibility of his arguments has in turn to depend on the individual's giving his assent. There is, as we urged at the outset an inescapable second-order responsibility for moral and political beliefs, which will always rest with the individual, so long as the notion of responsibility is not dissolved in some kind of determinism.

It is at the point at which we consider the powers and capabilities of the individual, that the clash between the frameworks of reference of the Marxist and the literal moralist become fundamentally irreconcilable, if it is felt that there is a point, however difficult to specify, at which the individual is 'free', and that interpretation, such as that given of Jim as an 'effect of system', leads to a determinism which rules out any question of moral blame, and hence makes otiose much of Marlow's speculation. The attack on the deterministic features of the Marxist position has been elo-quently expressed by his Isaiah Berlin in his *Four Essays on Liberty*.[38] However I do not think that this is really at issue in our discussion of interpretation, as the Marxist may admit the possibility of moral interpretation on liberal terms, and yet urge the superiority of his own on essentially pragmatic grounds.

Indeed Jameson seems to feel that ethical matters, even when we can be certain of them, are ultimately irrelevant to his larger purposes:

only an ethical politics, linked to those ethical categories we have often had occasion to criticize and deconstruct in the previous pages, will feel the need to 'prove' that one of these forms of class consciousness is good or positive and the other reprehensible or wicked : on the grounds, for example, that working-class consciousness is potentially more universal than ruling-class consciousness, or that the latter is essentially linked to violence or repression. It is unnecessary to argue these quite correct propositions; ideological commitment is not first and foremost a matter of moral choice but of the taking of sides in a struggle between embattled groups. (290)[39]

Such commitment urges us to go beyond the contrasting interpretations of the text as I have tried to describe them here, and return to that conflict of ends within the institutions of critical activity to which I alluded at the outset. For the variations in interpretative norms are further justified in so far as they are seen to promote the interests of different social groups. The interpreter may wish to align himself with 'progressive' forces. Thus Slaughter argues that the history of Marxist concern with literature is part of 'the long struggle to develop theory in the way that Marx conceived : in the creation of a revolutionary working-class movement'.[40] And Jameson argues, less vigorously perhaps, that the interpreter should 'rewrite the individual text, the individual cultural artefact in terms of the antagonistic dialogue of class voices' (85). In this way the hegemony of the bourgeois or ruling class world-view is attacked. However, it should be pointed out that, in terms of the logic of our oppositional model, a text which expresses the power relations of any *other* dominant group might be seen as having similarly indirect repressive aims. It is only the antecedent historical judgement concerning the relationship between classes in the society in question that licenses the Marxist analysis. For similar antagonisms may be similarly exposed, for example in the feminist analysis of patriarchy (which need not itself be subordinated to a Marxist point of view).[41] Exactly parallel arguments could be produced in analysis of the 'official literature' of a Marxist bureaucratic state, in say its relationship to the interests and desires of a dissenting intelligentsia; or in looking at the relationship of theologian and laity in eighteenth-century Europe in the period of what Peter Gay has called 'The Rise of Modern Paganism'.[42] My concentration on Marxist analysis in this chapter does not concede its right to dominance, as there is nothing to prevent us from using their logic for ideological interpretation to mount a parallel analysis of any requisitely disguised dominant ideology operative within any relatively closed culture. The decision to embark on one or the other type of analysis thus depends on an antecedent judgement as to the 'real' interests of particular social groups, and the desire to defend one against the other.

Marxist critical theory reminds interpreters of all political complexions that the implications of the text will depend on our specification (and indeed theorization) of its historical context. I thus agree with Bennett that Marxists have been rightly concerned to 'calculate the political effect' of the text as a 'specific practice of writing, bound, circumscribed and conditioned by the historical, material and ideological conditions of its production.'[43] This may well lead to the recovery of a regard for historical scholarship within theoretical criticism: Foucault succeeding Derrida, perhaps. Marxist interpretation also offers models for showing us how literature may (mis)represent the interests of social groupings, though not, as I have argued, with a monopoly on the practice, as Kate Millett's strictures on D. H. Lawrence, for example, will show.[44] The result of all this activity is, I think, a more profound though more relativist awareness on the part of the interpreter of the relationship of literature to belief. These crudely summarized tendencies within Marxist literary theory may I think inspire the liberal critic, even if he is disinclined to accept some of its associated notions—of the 'hidden narrative' of history, of the ultimate importance of class conflict (rather than that between individuals), and so on. Marxist analysis is also providing a series of challenges to the institutions of teaching that need to be debated. A reply needs to be given to those who argue that even apparently liberal modes of argument from within educational institutions may in fact and unawares, defuse and repress differences within society that deserve a more frank expression. But these speculations take us a long way beyond my original terms of reference, which centred on the search for the plausible linguistic implications of the text; and they will not be pursued any further here. They may nevertheless serve as a perhaps rather belated indication to the reader of the radical–liberal position from which the foregoing argument has been conducted; a position against which, no doubt, some of the arguments I have deployed above could themselves in turn be applied, despite my attempt to take on as self-critical a responsibility as I could manage for them.

Notes

Translations are by the author, except where|otherwise indicated

1 Implication

1. I refer here to the work of H. P. Grice, particularly his 'Logic and Conversation' in P. Cole and J. Morgan (eds.), *Syntax and Semantics 3: Speech Acts* (New York 1975). Grice argues that speaker/hearer relationships can be seen to be governed by maxims, for example that of the 'co-operative principle' which demands informativeness for the purpose of the exchange, truth-telling, relevance, and perspicuity. I believe these conditions to apply also to text/reader relationships, though they are only normally assumed to be in force. M. L. Pratt, who elaborates a Gricean theory of the text in her *Towards a Speech Act Theory of Literary Discourse* (London 1977), points out that the literary text is often most interesting when it violates or 'flouts' these principles, as obviously in *Tristram Shandy* (see her 135 ff., 152 ff. and 163 ff.).
2. N. Smith and D. Wilson, *Modern Linguistics; the results of Chomsky's Revolution* (Harmondsworth 1979), 148 ff. Cf. also T. Van Dijk, *Text and Context* (London 1977), 111 f.; and on the interplay between 'experiential' and logical systems cf. also M. A. K. Halliday, *Language as Social Semiotic* (London 1978), 130 ff.
3. Smith and Wilson, op.cit. 173.
4. Ibid. 178.
5. Henry James, *The Golden Bowl*, Book II, Ch.42.
6. On conversational implication and our knowledge of the personal history of the participants, cf. R. de Beaugrande, *Text Discourse and Process* (London 1980), 246 f.
7. Halliday, op.cit. 136. For the further contrast of conversation and text see his 140 f. Pratt on the other hand (op.cit., Ch.IV and *passim*), argues that conversational principles apply equally well to literary texts. See also Beaugrande (op.cit. VIII, 2, 242–54), on conversation. Browning's dramatic monologues offer some typical problems for the reader's construction of a cotext.
8. It comes from D. Rumelhart's 'Some Problems with the Notion of Literal Meaning' in A. Ortony (ed.), *Metaphor and Thought* (Cambridge 1979), 78 ff. His discussion differs from mine in many details, though I follow his basic strategy of analysis, 86 ff.
9. Ibid. 87.
10. Van Dijk, op.cit. 94.
11. Cf. van Dijk on condition consequence orderings, op.cit 105.
12. Ibid. 99.
13. Beaugrande, op.cit. 163 ff., giving references to the relevant literature. This corresponds in some degree to van Dijk's argument that we may order the facts within a frame along cause–consequence, general–particular, and whole–part lines, op.cit. 99.
14. Halliday, op.cit. 137.

15. Van Dijk, op.cit. 159 ff. On the use of frames in interpretation, see further U. Eco, *The Role of the Reader* (London 1981), 20 ff. He also reminds us of the 'intertextual' frame, where the frame in one narrative text is interpreted by us in terms of one familiar to us from other texts.
16. Van Dijk, op.cit. 49.
17. Ibid. 161.
18. Cf. Beaugrande, op.cit. 77–102, on 'Building the Text-world Model'.

2.1 Metaphor in the Text

1. Samuel Johnson, *Lives of the Poets* (1781), ed. G. B. Hill, ii (Oxford 1935), 128.
2. E. E. Cummings, *Collected Poems* (London 1968), I, 306.
3. Cf. Max Black's arguments against Donald Davidson in S. Sacks (ed.), *On Metaphor* (Chicago and London 1979), esp 182 ff., also van Dijk in M. K. L. Ching, M. C. Haley, and R. F. Lunsford, (eds.), *Linguistic Perspectives on Literature* (London 1980), 117 f., who adapts Grice to the analysis of metaphor as a speech act which appears to violate maxims like those of truth and relevance. A Gricean approach is however criticized by J. M. Sadock, in A. Ortony (ed.), *Metaphor and Thought* (Cambridge 1979), 56 ff.
4. Cf. John Searle in Ortony (ed.) op.cit. 94 ff., also his article, 'Literal Meaning', *Erkenntnis* 13 (1978), 204–44.
5. On the development of this ability see H. Gardner and E. Winner in Sacks, op.cit., esp. 125 ff., and for a survey of psychological studies see A. Paivio in Ortony (ed.), op.cit. 150 ff.
6. On foregrounding see G. N. Leech, *A Linguistic Guide to English Poetry* (London 1969), 56 f., and J. Mukarovsky in D. C. Freeman (ed.), *Linguistic and Literary Style* (London 1977), 40 ff.
7. See Max Black, *Models and Metaphors* (Cornell 1962), 28 ff. On the focusing interpretation of all sentences, see P. Pettit, *The Concept of Structuralism* (London 1979), 24 f.
8. As Ortony argues in op.cit. 191 ff.
9. Cf. Searle in Ortony (ed.), op.cit. 98 f. On irony as a prolegomenon to metaphor from this point of view see P. Werth in T. Eaton (ed.), *Essays in Literary Semantics* (Heidelberg 1978), 87 ff.
10. Cf. Black, op.cit. 40 f.
11. L. J. Cohen, in Ortony (ed.), op.cit. 70.
12. Cohen, ibid. 72–3.
13. For 'logical space' see van Dijk in Ching (ed.), op.cit. 120 ff., and for 'psycholexical space' cf. M. C. Haley in Ching (ed.), op.cit. 139 ff.
14. As Cohen points out, op.cit. 75, 'Lexical entries of a natural language can draw no clear distinction between features that are supposed to be "purely linguistic" and features that are supposed to represent common knowledge or commonly accepted beliefs.'
15. Cf. D. Bickerton, 43 ff., and M. J. Reddy, 63 ff., in Ching (ed.), op.cit.
16. M. J. Reddy, in Ching (ed.), op.cit. 66 ff.
17. Cf. P. Werth in Eaton (ed.), op.cit. 74.
18. G. N. Leech, op.cit., referring to Uriel Weinreich's 'Explorations in semantic theory' in *Current Trends in Linguistics*, Vol.3, ed. T. A. Seboek (The Hague, 1966), 455–71.
19. Leech, op.cit. 154 ff.
20. Ibid. 154.

21. Reinhart in Ching (ed.), op.cit. 98 ff.
22. Ibid. 99. Cf. Werth in Eaton (ed.), op.cit. 84.
23. Searle in Ortony (ed.), op.cit. 106.
24. Ibid. 99.
25. Cf. Searle, ibid. 116 ff., whom I follow here. He discriminates eight different principles for 'calling to mind'.
26. P. Henle (ed.), *Language Thought and Culture* (Ann Arbor 1965), 186.
27. On the indeterminacy of the referential commitments of metaphor, cf. Reddy in Ching (ed.), op.cit. 68–75, and G. N. Leech, *Towards a Semantic Description of English* (London 1969), 80 ff. and esp. 92.
28. Cf. Black in Ortony (ed.) op.cit. 42.
29. See Thomas Parkinson, *Yeats: the Later Poetry* (Berkeley and Los Angelos 1964), 103.
30. Parkinson, ibid. 101 ff., discusses the MS evolution of this whole stanza.

2.2 Metaphor in the Language

1. T. E. Hulme, 'Cinders' in *Speculations*, 2nd edn., ed. H. Read (London 1936), 233 f.
2. Jacques Derrida, 'White Mythology', *New Literary History*, Vol.VI (1974), No.1, 5–74. Translated from *Poétique* 5 (1971), 1–52, and reprinted in *Marges de la philosophie* (Paris 1972), 247–324.
3. Ibid. 9.
4. P. B. Shelley, *A Defence of Poetry* (1820), reprinted in *English Critical Essays of the Nineteenth Century*, ed. E. D. Jones (Oxford 1947), 104 f.
5. Derrida, op.cit. 11.
6. Ibid. 12.
7. Ibid. 12.
8. Paul Ricœur, *La Métaphore vive* (Paris 1975), 363. 'Heideggerian deconstruction must now take on Nietzschean genealogy, Freudian psychoanalysis, the Marxist critique of ideology, that is, the weapons of the hermeneutics of suspicion. Armed in this way, the critique is capable of unmasking the *unthought* conjunction of *hidden* metaphysics and *worn-out* metaphor.' (Paul Ricœur, *The Rule of Metaphor*, trans. Robert Czerny, London 1978, 285.)
9. Derrida, op.cit. 12.
10. Ibid. 23. Derrida analyses examples, particularly from Aristotle (30–46), but his use of the sun as a central metaphor (43 ff.) is most peculiar.
11. Ricœur, op.cit. 364.
12. Derrida, op.cit. 48.
13. Ibid. 24.
14. Ricœur, op.cit. 368.
15. Ibid. 369. Cf. Wittgenstein's notion of 'meaning in use'. 'There is no need for a metaphysic of the proper to justify the difference between literal and figurative. It is use in discourse that specifies the difference between the literal and the metaphorical and not some sort of prestige attributed to the primitive or the original.' (Trans. R. Czerny, op.cit. 291.)
16. Cf. L. Wittgenstein, *Philosophical Investigations* (Oxford 1953), para.151, and G. Pitcher, *The Philosophy of Wittgenstein* (Englewood Cliffs 1964), 270–5.
17. G. Lakoff and M. Johnson, *Metaphors We Live By* (Chicago and London 1980). Cf. similar work by M. J. Reddy on the 'conduit' metaphor for communication reported in A. Ortony (ed.), *Metaphor and Thought* (Cambridge 1979), 284–324.

18. Lakoff and Johnson, op.cit. 46 and 52 f.
19. Ibid. 7 ff.
20. For their fuller discussion see ibid. 85 ff. on love as journey, and 89–96 for their discussion of argument as journey.
21. Ibid. 119 f.
22. Ibid. 122.
23. Cf. ibid. 159.
24. Ibid. 179 and cf. 193 f.
25. This accords with the arguments of many analytical philosophers in the Dewey–Wittgenstein tradition, that even 'ordinary language is not a single "conceptual scheme", but a motley of conceptual schemes, of "versions", of "worlds" '. Hilary Putman, 'On Convention', *New Literary History* Vol.XIII (1981), No.1, 7, referring us to Nelson Goodman, *Ways of Worldmaking* (Indianapolis 1978).
26. Cf. Lakoff and Johnson, op.cit. 181 and 186 ff.
27. Cf. ibid, 211 ff.
28. The metaphorical structuring of our thinking is best shown perhaps in historical studies : for example, in M. H. Abrams, *The Mirror and the Lamp* (Oxford 1953), *passim*, but perhaps especially so in Ch.III on 'Romantic analogues of art and mind'. Metaphorical structuring within the text is of course typical of allegory : a novel like John Barth's *Giles Goat-Boy* (1966), for example, depends upon an ingenious equation between the university and the world. Cf. Robert Scholes's analysis in *Fabulation and Metafiction* (Chicago and London 1979), 75–104. See also Eugenio Donato's discussion of the underlying metaphors of library and museum in Flaubert's *Bouvard and Pécuchet* in his 'The Museum Furnace' in Josué V. Harari (ed.), *Textual Strategies: perspectives in poststructuralist criticism* (London 1980), 213 ff.

3.1 Linguistics and Interpretation

1. E. E. Cummings, Poem LI of '1 Times 1' in *Complete Poems 1936–1962* (London 1968), 594.
2. The 'subliminal' view is close to that of Jakobson in his discussion of parallelism and equivalence; see his *Questions de poétique* (Paris 1973), 272 f.
3. On the problem of the psychological reality of the rules and principles reported by linguists, cf. N. Smith and D. Wilson, *Modern Linguistics* (Harmondsworth 1977), 21–6.
4. Cf. John Lyons, *Semantics I* (Cambridge 1977), 230 ff. Accounts of Saussure are standard within structuralist criticism, e.g. J. Culler, *Structuralist Poetics* (London 1975) Ch.1, 3–31; T. Hawkes, *Structuralism and Semiotics* (London 1977), 19–28. My account here is very selective. For a good discussion of the distinctions here at issue, see P. Pettit, *The Concept of Structuralism* (Berkeley and London 1977), Ch.1, 1–29.
5. F. de Saussure, *Cours de linguistique générale* 5th. edn. (Paris 1960), 170 ff.
6. I take the term from Lyons, op.cit. 248.
7. On the ideological significance of gender distinctions, see e.g. G. Kress and R. Hodge, *Language as Ideology* (London 1979), 77–82.
8. See Peter Jones, *Philosophy and the Novel* (Oxford 1975), Ch.1.
9. Cf. T. Todorov, *Poétique* (Paris 1967), 19 ff.
10. R. Hasan, 'Code register and dialect' in B. Bernstein, *Class Codes and Control*, Vol.2 (London 1973), 258.

11. M. A. K. Halliday, *Language as Social Semiotic* (London 1978), 111. Cf. also B. Martin, *A Sociology of Contemporary Cultural Change* (Oxford 1981), Ch.3, 27 ff., esp. 36 ff.

12. Problems also arise when we make synchronic comparisons between different cultures' discourses within the same field, and when we look diachronically at the history of their development; see S. Ullman, *Language and Style* (Oxford 1964), 222 ff.

13. Saussure, op.cit. 160. 'Within the same language, all words used to express related ideas limit each other reciprocally; synonyms like French *redouter* 'dread', *craindre* 'fear', and *avoir peur* 'be afraid' have value only through their opposition; if *redouter* did not exist, all its content would go to its competitors' (F. de Saussure, *Course in General Linguistics* trans. Wade Baskin, London 1974, 116.)

14. As we have suggested, the mode of existence of such fields is very difficult to describe. They may depend upon associative psychology (though Guiraud found the minimum associative field for *chat* ran to 300 words, as reported S. Ullman, *Semantics* (Oxford 1962), 240). Or they can simply be theoretically ascribed to the 'langue' which notionally underlies 'parole'. See Ullman, op.cit. 238 ff.

15. For a typically brilliant and uncompromising example, see R. Barthes, *Elements of Semiology* (Paris 1964) and his *Système de la mode* (Paris 1967). This use of the methods of linguistics for the analysis of cultural artefacts is critically discussed by Pettit, op.cit. 36 ff. In literary cases, the aim was to say that narrative was like a single expanded sentence; cf. R. Barthes 'The structural analysis of narrative' reprinted and translated in S. Heath (ed.), *Image–Music–Text* (London, 1977), 79–124, discussed by Fowler, *Linguistics and the Novel* (London 1977), *passim*, and Pettit, op.cit. 47 f., who points out the disanalogies here.

16. J. Culler, *Structuralist Poetics* (London 1975,), 5. On the real complexities of such constitutive rules, see J. Searle, *Speech Acts* (Cambridge 1969), 33–42, and *passim*.

17. J. Culler, op.cit. 259.

18. Cf. e.g. J. Culler, *The Pursuit of Signs* (London 1981), 37 f., with R. S. Crane *The Language of Criticism and the Structure of Poetry* (Toronto 1953), 123 f.

19. The reader might like to compare the changing theoretical assumptions about semantic fields and codes in this respect in Winifred Nowottny's analysis of a Shakespeare sonnet in *The Language Poets Use* (London 1962), 76–85, Culler's of Blake's 'London', in Hilda Schiff (ed.), *Contemporary Approaches to English Studies* (London 1977), 72 ff., and *Pursuit of Signs* op.cit. 68–79, and M. Riffaterre's of a poem by Queneau in his *Semiotics of Poetry* (London 1980), 105 ff.

20. R. Kuhns, 'Semantics for literary languages', *New Literary History* Vol.IV (1972), No.1, 102. Linguists have shown a growing interest in the 'beyond the sentence' cohesion of literary texts. Cf. e.g. Halliday op.cit., on a Thurber fable, Ch.7, 128–53 and Roger Fowler, *Literature as Social Discourse* (London 1981), 68 ff., on the same text.

21. Cf. R. Barthes, op.cit. ; J. Culler on Joyce's 'Eveline' in *Structuralist Poetics*, op.cit. 221 ff.; and R. Scholes on the same story in his *Semiotics and Interpretation* (New Haven and London 1982), 87–109.

22. J. Culler, op.cit. 126. He appreciates the problems I shall now raise concerning competence: cf his pp. 113–30.

23. Cf. Kuhns, op.cit. 95 f., who defines basic competence in my sense as the ability to deal with the determination of semantic structure (ambiguities etc.), as the formal reading of the text as morphological, sequential, or relational,

and as our awareness of the ontological reading of the text—its relation to systems of belief and rules of denotation.

24. R. Barthes, *Critique et vérité* (Paris 1966), on 'La science de la littérature', 56 ff., and 'La critique', 63 ff.

3.2 Leda and the Swan

1. M. A. K. Halliday, 'Descriptive linguistics and literary studies', Ch.3 of M. A. K. Halliday and A. McIntosh, *Patterns of Language* (London 1966), 56 ff.
2. Ibid. 60. Rankshift happens 'when a given unit is as it were "shifted" down the rank scale to operate as a part of the pattern of one further down or of equal value to itself': M. A. K. Halliday, A. McIntosh, and P. Strevens, *The Linguistic Sciences and Language Teaching* (London 1964), 27.
3. Halliday, ibid. 61.
4. Cf. ibid. 60.
5. But for purposes of comparison see e.g. C. Brooke-Rose, *A Grammar of Metaphor* (London 1958), Ch.9, 'The Verb'; and Rulon Wells, 'Nominal and verbal style' in T. A. Sebeok (ed.), *Style in Language* (Boston 1960), 213–20.
6. And indeed in the Russian Formalists in general. See V. Erlich, *Russian Formalism* (The Hague 1955), T. Bennett, *Formalism and Marxism* (London 1979), Part One, and F. Jameson *The Prison House of Language* (Princeton 1972), 43–100. On Jakobson see Culler, *Structuralist Poetics* (London 1975), 55–75. I follow him here.
7. R. Jakobson, 'Linguistics and Poetics' in Sebeok, op.cit. 357.
8. See T. Todorov, 'Some approaches to Russian Formalism' in S. Bann and S. Bowlt (eds.), *Russian Formalism* (Edinburgh 1973), 7 f.
9. J. Culler, op.cit. 57. Cf. P. Pettit, *The Concept of Structuralism* (Berkeley and London 1977), 40 ff., who proposes to correct this by a principle of 'reflective equilibrium' from John Rawls : 'The stylistic analysis of a poem, the account of significant patterns within the poem and its effects, must be in equilibrium with our intuitive sense of what effects matter in that poem and poems of its sort', p.41. But this simply readmits the generic expectations of the critic into the linguistic analysis. The method and results of Jakobsonian analysis have been much criticized : see in addition to Culler, op.cit. M.-L. Pratt, *Towards a Speech Act Theory of Literature* (Bloomington and London 1977), 29–37, Roger Fowler, *Literature as Social Discourse* (London 1981), Ch.9, 162 ff., who argues that Jakobson's analyses are 'notoriously shallow, formalistic, dominated by mechanical and perhaps spurious patterns in phonology and syntax, absolutely uniformative when the analyst comes to interpretation or to placing in history' (p.167), and David Robey, in Ann Jefferson and D. Robey (eds.), *Modern Literary Theory* (London 1982), 49 ff.
10. R. Jakobson, 'Poetry of grammar and grammar of poetry', *Lingua*, 21 (1968), 602.
11. Jakobson asserts that 'Rhyme necessarily involves the semantic relationship between rhyming units', in Sebeok, op.cit. 367. Further 'in poetry any suspicious similarity to sound is evaluated in respect to similarity or dissimilarity in meaning', ibid. 372. Note the mood of the verbs here.
12. Wolfgang Iser's analyses of the reading process are in some ways relevant here, although he concentrates more on prose. Cf. his remarks on 'the structure of theme and horizon' in *The Act of Reading* (Baltimore 1978), 96 ff. An account of the psychology of the reading process (and how little we know

about it) is offered by G. Cohen, 'The Psychology of Reading' in *New Literary History* Vol.IV (1972), No.1, 75 ff.

13. G. Hartman, *Criticism in the Wilderness* (New Haven 1980), 23.
14. Ibid. 21.

4 The Text and the External World

1. J. Culler, *Structuralist Poetics* (London 1975), 53.
2. Iris Murdoch, *Sartre* (London 1965), 50 f.
3. T. Hawkes, *Structuralism and Semiotics* (London 1977), 17. For similar statements cf. David Robey and Ann Jefferson (eds.), in their *Modern Literary Theory* (London 1982), 46 and 86. The former sees the literary text as a linguistic structure whose 'connection' with the real world is 'purely arbitrary' (which does not say much for the intentions of language users), and the latter thinks that the structuralist thus 'sets aside all questions of content' (an impossible task where language is concerned). Such statements have acquired the status of dogma in recent literary theory, and show a peculiar reluctance to think through the consequences of views attributed to Saussure.
4. For example, in interpreting Henry James's 'The Turn of the Screw'.
5. T. Todorov, 'Introduction : Le vraisemblable', *Communications*, II (1968), 2 f. Cited by Culler, op.cit. 139.
6. M. Riffaterre, 'Interpretation and descriptive poetry', *New Literary History* Vol.IV (1973), No.2, 229–56. Further page references are given in the text.
7. This gives rise to a general theory of poetry which Riffaterre elaborates in his *Semiotics of Poetry* (London 1980). This is criticized severely by R. Fowler, *Literature as Social Discourse* (London 1981), 131 ff., and by J. Culler, *The Pursuit of Signs* (London 1981), 91 ff.
8. Such a mimetic theory is found e.g. in W. J. Harvey, *Character and the Novel* (London 1965).
9. M.-L. Pratt, *Towards a Speech Act Theory of Literature* (Bloomington and London 1977), 91 f.
10. Cf. John Reichert, 'Do Poets ever mean what they say?', *New Literary History*, Vol.XIII (1981), No.1, 53 ff.
11. L. Goldman, *Le Dieu caché* (Paris 1959).
12. R. Barthes, *S/Z* (Paris 1970), 4. Further references in the text. Cf. for studies of the novel, R. Fowler *Linguistics and the Novel* (London 1977), G. Genette, *Narrative Discourse* (Oxford 1980), R. Scholes, *Semiotics and Interpretation* (New Haven and London 1982), and also U. Eco, 'Narrative structures in Fleming', in his *Role of the Reader* (London 1981), Ch.6, 144 ff.
13. Barthes has a peculiar distinction between the 'réel' and the 'opérable' based on the question: what if the reader were to attempt to perform Marianina's 'roulade adorable admirablement bien executée'?, *S/Z*, op.cit. 87 ff. 'To depict is to unroll the carpet of the codes, to refer not from a language to a referent but from one code to another. Thus realism . . . consists not in copying the real, but in copying a (depicted) copy of the real.' (Barthes, *S/Z*, trans. R. Miller, London 1975, 55).
14. These are the proaeretic, governing the construal of plot based on expectation; the hermeneutic, governing the questions raised in the mind of the reader—enigmas, suspense, and so on; the semic, which organizes the central semantic features governing longer passages; the symbolic, which allows for our extrapolation to thematic readings; and the referential code which

summarizes the cultural background of the text. They are discussed by Hawkes, op.cit. 116 ff.

15. R. Barthes, *Critical Essays* (Evanston 1972), 258.
16. Cf. Hawkes, op.cit. 119, who points out that the other codes could easily be construed as mere aspects of the referential one. Barthes has partly met this criticism by modifying the arguments of *S/Z* in his 'Textual analysis of Poe's *Valdemar*', in R. Young (ed.), *Untying the Text* (London 1981), 155 ff. The codes are described here as simply 'associative' and as 'essentially cultural' (155).
17. J. Culler, *Structuralist Poetics* (London 1975), 142, suggests that the substitution of 'painter' or 'teacher' here will show the force of this.
18. 'There, milling about, whirling around, flitting here and there, were the most beautiful women of Paris, the richest, the noblest, dazzling, stately, resplendent with diamonds, flowers in their hair, on their bosoms, on their heads, strewn over dresses or in garlands at their feet. Light, rustling movements and voluptuous steps, made the laces, the silk brocades, the gauzes, float around their delicate forms.' (Trans. R. Miller, op.cit. 25).
19. 'Allusively an adulterous ambiance is indicated; it connotes Paris as an immoral city (Parisian fortunes, the Lanty's included, are immoral).' (Ibid.)
20. 'From a body of knowledge, from an anonymous book whose best model is doubtless the School Manual.' (Ibid. 205.)
21. 'Although entirely derived from books [these codes] by a swivel characteristic of bourgeois ideology, which turns culture into nature, appear to establish reality, "Life". "Life" then, in the classic text, becomes a nauseating mixture of current opinions, a smothering layer of received ideas; in fact it is in these cultural codes that what is outmoded in Balzac, the essence of what in Balzac cannot be (re)written, is concentrated.' (Ibid. 206).
22. R. Fowler, *Literature as Social Discourse* op.cit. 96 ff.
23. For a discussion of this distinction between meaning and significance, cf. E. D. Hirsch, *Validity in Interpretation* (New Haven 1967), 8 ff., 62 ff., 140 ff., and his *Aims of Interpretation* (Chicago 1976), Ch.1, 1–17.
24. L. W. Tancock (ed.), *Germinal* (Harmondsworth 1954), 13. Cf. F. W. J. Hemmings, *Émile Zola* (Oxford 1970), 186–211.
25. F. R. Leavis, *D. H. Lawrence Novelist* (Harmondsworth 1964), 115.
26. Ibid.
27. Ibid. 138.
28. Ibid. 150.

5.1 Deconstruction and Scepticism

1. R. Rorty. *Philosophy and the Mirror of Nature* (Oxford 1980), 315. We have already seen how contributions to a discourse may be incommensurable in our discussion of metaphor.
2. Jacques Derrida, *Positions* (Paris 1972), 30. Cf. also his *De la Grammatologie* (Paris 1967), 36 ff.
3. Derrida, *Positions*, op.cit. 23. Cf. his *La Dissémination* (Paris 1972), 108.
4. G. Hartman, *Saving the Text* (Baltimore and London 1981), 4.
5. J. Derrida, op.cit. 37 f. 'Whether it occurs in spoken or written discourse no element can function as a sign without referring us back to another element which itself is not simply present. This linkage ensures that each 'element'—phoneme or grapheme—is constituted from the beginning by the trace within it of the other elements in the sequence or system.'

6. 'The bourgeois or neurotic . . .is unable to live within this pure temporality of difference and must ultimately have recourse to some comforting doctrine of a transcendental signified at whatever level, whether it be that of God, political authority, machismo, the literary work, or simply meaning itself.' F. Jameson, *The Prison House of Language* (Princeton 1972), 182, reporting the view of the *Tel Quel* group.

7. J. Derrida, op.cit. 17.

8. J. Derrida, 'Différance' in *Speech and Phenomena* translated by David B. Allison (Evanston 1973), 138, 140.

9. J. Derrida, *L'Écriture et la différence* (Paris 1967 : reprinted 1979) 412. 'We cannot state any destructive proposition which has not already had to slip into the form, the logic, and the hidden assumptions, of that very proposition which it wishes to dispute. To take an example from among so many : it is with the help of the concept of the sign that we disturb the metaphysics of presence.'

10. J. Derrida, *Positions*, op.cit. 50. 'Grammatology would be no doubt not so much another science, or a new discipline charged with a new content and a new well marked-out domain, as the vigilant practice of this textual division'.

11. Cf. J. Derrida, *De la grammatologie*, op.cit. 42–6, 51–63; and J. Culler's discussion of this topic, *On Deconstruction* (London 1983), 100 ff.

12. Derrida adduces similar arguments against Lévi-Strauss. Cf. C. Norris, *Deconstruction* (London 1982), 37 ff.

13. Cf. G. Graff, *Literature Against Itself* (Chicago 1979), *passim*, and esp. 61 f., 81 f., 192 f.

14. J. Derrida, *L'Écriture et la différence*, op.cit. 34. 'Our discourse belongs irreducibly to the system of metaphysical oppositions. One cannot announce the rupture of this belonging except by a *certain* organization, a certain *strategic* ordering, which, inside the field of its own powers, turning against itself its own strategems, produces a force of dislocation which spreads right across the system, fissuring it in all directions and delimiting it through and through.'

5.2 Ambiguity and Self-contradiction

1. H. Levin, *The Gates of Horn* (New York 1966), 66.

2. Cf. Michael Foucault, 'What is an Author?' in J. V. Harari (ed.), *Textual Strategies* (London 1980), 141 ff., and R. Barthes, 'The Death of the Author' in S. Heath (ed.), *Image–Music–Text* (London 1977), 142 ff. I have discussed some of the consequences of their positions in my 'Joyce and the Displaced author' in W. J. McCormack and A. Stead (eds.), *James Joyce and Modern Literature* (London 1982).

3. G. Graff, *Literature Against Itself* (Chicago and London 1979), 145 f. Thus J.Culler tells us that *Madame Bovary* is ultimately 'about' signs and meaning, and that Blake's 'London' narrates 'acts of interpretation, a reading of signs', in *The Pursuit of Signs* (London 1981), 36.

4. G. Graff, op.cit. 175 ff., referring to J. Hillis Miller, 'The Function of Realism: Sketches by Boz, Oliver Twist, and Cruikshank's Illustrations' in *Dickens : Centennial Essays*, ed. A. Nisbet and B. Nevius (Berkeley 1971), 85 ff.

5. G. Graff, op.cit. 177.

6. Hillis Miller, op.cit. 122.

7. G. Graff, op.cit. 175.

8. Hillis Miller, op.cit. 116.

9. Cf. G. Graff, op.cit. 176.

10. P. de Man, 'Semiology and Rhetoric' cited from J. V. Harari (ed.), op.cit. 132. Further references in the text.

11. On this distinction, cf. D. Lodge, *The Modes of Modern Writing* (London 1977), esp. 73 ff., and for an argument parallel to de Man's attempting to show the underlying connection between metaphorical and metonymic, see U. Eco, *The Role of the Reader* (London 1981), 67 ff.

12. Marcel Proust, *A la recherche du temps perdu* (Paris 1954), I, 83. I use de Man's own translation here.

13. On this distinction and the article as a whole, cf. F. Lentricchia, *After the New Criticism* (London 1980), 314 ff.

14. For a similar line of argument, cf. J. Culler, op.cit. 190 ff.

15. Cf. e.g. A. G. Lehmann, *The Symbolist Aesthetic in France 1885–1895* (Oxford 1968), Ch.3, 'Poetic Knowledge', 74 ff.

16. Cf. C. Norris, *Deconstruction* (London 1982), 19.

17. P. de Man, *Allegories of Reading* (New Haven and London 1979), 115.

18. Cf. F. Lentricchia, op.cit. 182 ff., and 299 ff.

19. P. de Man, op.cit. 247.

20. J.-J. Rousseau, in B. Gagnebin and M. Raymond (eds.), *Œuvres complètes* (Paris 1959), I, 86.

21. P. de Man, op.cit. 280. Further references are given in the text.

22. P. de Man, in Harari (ed.), op.cit. 139.

23. B. Johnson's readings in *The Critical Difference* (Baltimore and London 1980), 61 ff., are especially relevant in the context of deconstruction.

24. B. Johnson, op.cit. x f. Further references are given in the text.

25. Herman Melville, *Billy Budd, Sailor and other Stories* ed. H. Beaver (Harmondsworth 1967), 380. I have argued elsewhere that the clash between irreconcilable viewpoints, so as to put the audience in a state of real doubt, is characteristic of tragedy, cf. C. Butler, 'Tragedy and Moral Education' in H. Schiff (ed.), *Contemporary Approaches to English Studies* (London 1977), 77–93.

26. Alain Robbe-Grillet, *Pour un nouveau roman* (Paris 1963), 36. 'Their ready-made idea of reality . . . invention and imagination may finally become the subject of the book.'

27. 'Prière d'insérer' for *Project pour un revolution à New York* (Paris 1970), reprinted from an article in *Le Nouvel Observateur*, 26 June 1970. I discuss the implied aesthetic here in my *After the Wake* (Oxford 1980), 38 ff. For a more extensive treatment of the matters raised here, cf. U. Eco, op.cit., Ch.1, 'The Poetics of the Open Work', 47 ff. 'The anecdote sets about growing; discontinuing, plural, mobile, subject to chance, pointing out its own fictitiousness, it becomes a "game" in the strongest sense of the word.'

5.3 Free Play

1. J. Derrida, 'Structure sign and play' in R. Mackesey and E. Donato (eds.), *The Structuralist Controversy* (Baltimore 1972), 284. I quote this passage in English as in this form it has been the most influential of Derrida's texts, particularly in the United States.

2. R. Barthes, *S/Z* (Paris 1970), 10. 'The goal of literary work is to make the reader no longer a consumer, but a producer of the text.' (Barthes, *S/Z*, trans. R. Miller, London 1975, 4.)

3. Ibid. 11, 12. 'To interpret a text is not to give it a (more or less justified, more or less free) meaning, but in the contrary to appreciate what *plural* constitutes

it . . . in the ideal text, the networks are many and interact . . . a galaxy of signifiers.' (Ibid. 5.)

4. Ibid. 12.

5. Ibid. 19. 'To take this entrance is to aim, ultimately, not at a legal structure of norms and departures, a narrative of poetic Law, but at a perspective (of fragments, of voices from other texts, other codes) whose vanishing point is nonetheless ceaselessly pushed back, mysteriously opened.' (Trans. R. Miller, op.cit. 12.)

6. Ibid. 16. Cf. Derrida, 'La subjectivité—comme l'objectivité—est un effet de différence, un effet inscrit dans un système de différence', *Positions* (Paris 1972), 40. 'This "I" which approaches the text is already itself a plurality of other texts, of codes which are infinite . . . or lost.' (Trans. R. Miller, op.cit. 10.)

7. Barthes, op.cit. 18. Such readings are made 'pour multiplier les signifiants' (ibid. 171). This is not of course an acceptable consequence for a Marxist critic like T. Eagleton, who would see the interpreter's subjectivity in another light: 'The notion that the text is simply a ceaselessly self-signifying practice, whether source or object, stands four square with the bourgeois mythology of individual freedom', (*Criticism and Ideology* (London 1976), 73). 'Reading does not consist in stopping the chain of systems, in establishing a truth'. (Trans. R. Miller, op.cit. 11.)

8. J. Derrida, *De la Grammatologie* (Paris 1967), 74. 'From the very opening of the game then we are within the becoming unmotivated of the symbol . . . the immotivation of the trace ought now to be understood as an operation and not as a state, as an active movement, a demotivation, and not as a given structure.' (Derrida, *Of Grammatology*, trans. G. C. Spivak, London 1976, 50, 51.)

9. J. V. Harari, in Harari (ed.), *Textual Strategies* (London 1980), 30. He reprints a translation of 'The supplement of copula' in ibid. 82–120.

10. J. Derrida, 'Living On: Border Lines', in H. Bloom *et al.*, *Deconstruction and Criticism* (London 1979), 75. Subsequent references are given in the text.

11. E. D. Hirsch, *Aims of Interpretation* (Chicago 1976), 25.

12. Part of the answer to the question I ask is 'Dissemination' which is intended to break down semantic hierarchies, cf. Derrida, *Positions*, op.cit. 62, and *La Dissémination* (Paris 1972). Another answer, given by F. Lentricchia, *After the New Criticism* (London 1980), 168 f., is that Derrida's playful strategies subserve a central hedonist conception of value.

5.4 Norms for Interpretation

1. B. Barnes, *T. S. Kuhn and Social Science* (London 1982), 24.

2. For a discussion of overtly subjective interpretation cf. e.g. N. H. Holland, *The Dynamics of Literary Response* (New York 1968), and D. Bleich, *Subjective Criticism* (Baltimore and London 1978). The norms involved here are those of dynamic psychotherapy.

3. R. Rorty, 'Philosophy as a kind of writing : An essay on Derrida, *New Literary History*, Vol.X (Autumn 1978), No.1, 141–60, reprinted in his *Consequences of Pragmatism* (Brighton 1982), 90–109.

4. J. Derrida, *Positions* (Paris 1972), 48. 'Grammatology must deconstruct everything which . . . ties the concept and the norms of science to ontotheology logocentrism and phonologism. That is an immense and interminable task.'

5. On commensurability, cf. R. Rorty, *Philosophy and the Mirror of Nature* (Oxford 1980), 315 ff.

6. C. Altieri 'The Hermeneutics of literary indeterminacy', *New Literary History*, Vol.X (1978), No.1, 82.

7. J. Derrida, *De la Grammatologie* (Paris 1967), 227. 'Reading . . . cannot legitimately transgress the text towards something other than it, toward the referent (a reality that is metaphysical, historical, psychobiographical, etc.) or toward a signified outside the text whose content could take place, could have taken place outside of language, that is to say, in the sense that we give here to the word, outside of writing in general . . . There is nothing outside of the text [there is no outside-text].' (Derrida, *Of Grammatology* trans. G. C. Spivak, London 1978, 158.)

8. C. Norris, *Deconstruction* (London 1982), 84.

9. Cf. R. Rorty, *Consequences*, op.cit. xxv. He cites William James, *Pragmatism and the Meaning of Truth* (Cambridge, Mass. 1978), 42 : 'If the pragmatist is advised that he must confuse the *advisability of asserting* S with the *truth* of S, he will respond that the advice is question begging. The question is precisely whether "the true" is more than what William James defined it as : "The name of whatever proves itself to be good in the way of belief, and good, too, for definite assignable reasons".' It will be seen from this line of argument and what follows that I do not agree with J. Culler, *On Deconstruction* (London 1983), 153 ff., that deconstruction cannot be identified with pragmatism; since I think that all good arguments can. Even though Culler correctly points out that deconstructivists have a particular sympathy for arguments which attack accepted norms ('what has been excluded', 153) and try 'to keep alive the possibility that the eccentricity of women, poets, prophets and madmen might yield truths about the systems to which they are marginal' (154), I do not see how these 'truths' once urged, can avoid appealing to a (new) consensual group with pragmatic ends. Culler is thus wrong to suggest (154) that pragmatism may lead to complacency. Far from it.

10. J. Derrida, in H. Bloom *et al.*, *Deconstruction and Criticism* (London 1979), 166.

11. B. Barnes, op.cit. 17.

12. J. L. Austin, *How to do Things with Words* (Oxford 1962), 142–4.

13. D. C. Hoy, *The Critical Circle* (Berkeley and Los Angeles 1978), 167.

14. R. Rorty, *Philosophy and the Mirror of Nature*, op.cit. 170. Cf. Hoy, op.cit. 69.

15. R. Rorty, op.cit. 170. Cf. 174 ff., 179.

16. Cf. G. Highet, *The Classical Tradition* (Oxford 1949), 92–3, referring to G. Comparetti, *Vergil in the Middle Ages* (London 1895), Ch.7.

17. The historical aspect of this has become the province of 'reception theory' as pursued by Jauss, of whom Hoy gives an excellent account in op.cit. 150–9.

18. R. Rorty, *Consequences*, op.cit. 97 f.

19. Ibid. 98.

20. e.g. Josué V. Harari (ed.), *Textual Strategies* (London 1980) and R. Young (ed.), *Untying the Text* (London 1981).

21. J. Derrida, *Positions*, op.cit. 14.

22. R.Rorty, op.cit. 108.

23. Most explicitly perhaps in the work of G. Hartman, cf. his *Criticism in the Wilderness* (New Haven and London 1980), esp. Ch.8, 'Literary commentary as literature', 189 ff.

24. Attacked by G. Graff, *Literature Against Itself* (Chicago and London 1972), received with qualified approval by F. Lentricchia, *After the New Criticism* (London 1980), and celebrated by P. Widdowson (ed.) and others in *Re-Reading English* (London 1982).

6.1 Ideology and Opposition

1. The text itself may be adapted to institutional use, e.g. when edited for school pupils, Cf. R. Balibar, 'An example of literary work in France : George Sand's 'La Mare au diable'/'The Devil's Pool' of 1846', in F. Barker *et al.* (eds.), *The Sociology of Literature: 1848* (Colchester 1978), discussed in T. Bennett, *Formalism and Marxism* (London 1978), 158 ff.
2. Cf. E. D. Hirsch, *The Aims of Interpretation* (Chicago 1976), 120. On the law, see in particular, S. C. Yeazell, 'Convention, Fiction and the Law', *New Literary History*, Vol.XIII (1981), No.1, 89 ff.
3. On advice, cf. D. P. Gauthier, *Practical Reasoning* (Oxford 1963), Ch.5, 66 ff.
4. R. Geuss, *The Idea of a Critical Theory* (Cambridge 1981), 23.
5. Ibid. 22.
6. This line of judgement is particularly associated with the work of Jurgen Habermas, cf. R. Geuss, ibid. 12 ff., 31.
7. Ibid. 14.
8. Ibid. 20 ff.
9. Cf. Ibid., *passim* and esp. 26 ff.
10. Cf. T. Eagleton, *Criticism and Ideology* (London 1976), 44–63, and B. Sharratt, *Reading Relations* (Brighton 1982), 57 ff., for a discussion of Marxist models of literary activity in society.
11. For a study of the (peculiarly negative) relationship of English novelists in the nineteenth century to political institutions, see G. Watson, *The English Ideology* (London 1973).
12. For the relationship of ideology to conceptions of human nature cf. e.g. E. Fischer, *Art Against Ideology* (London 1969), esp. 77–134.
13. The letter of June 1956 is reprinted in A. Camus, *Théâtre, récits, nouvelles*, ed. R. Quillot (Paris, Pléiade 1962), 1973 ff.
14. Cf. C. C. O'Brien, *Camus* (London 1970), 47 ff.
15. P. Thody, *Albert Camus* (London 1961), 106.
16. D. Caute, *The Illusion* (London 1972), 81.
17. Cf. the account in J. Cruickshank, *Albert Camus and the Literature of Revolt* (London 1959), 120 ff.
18. J.-P. Sartre, *What is Literature?*, translated by B. Frechtman (London 1950), 14.
19. George Orwell, *The Road to Wigan Pier* (Harmondsworth 1962), 93. Cf. 116 f.
20. Compare the account of coal-picking in South Wales in the same period, in N. Branson and M. Heinemann, *Britain in the 1930s* (London 1973), 67. On the relationship of historical narrative to evidence, cf. A. C. Danto, *Analytical Philosophy of History* (Cambridge 1965), Chs.4 and 6.
21. For a discussion of this distinction and of I. A. Richard's attempts to eradicate it, cf. my 'I. A. Richards and the fortunes of critical theory', *Essays in Criticism*, Vol.XXX (July 1980), No.3, 198 ff.
22. On generalizations, see R. Fowler, *Literature as Social Discourse* (London 1981), Ch.6 *passim*, and also his *Linguistics and the Novel* (London 1977), 84–9.
23. I. A. Richards, *Practical Criticism* (1929; reprinted London 1964), 278.
24. T. S. Eliot, 'Shakespeare and the stoicism of Seneca' (1927), in his *Selected Essays* (London 1951), 137.
25. Ibid. 258.
26. For a discussion of the New Criticism and its ideological implications, cf. e.g. F. Mulhern, *The Moment of Scrutiny* (London 1979), and J. Fekete, *The Critical Twilight* (London 1978).

6.2 Hidden Ideology

1. R. Barthes, *S/Z* (Paris 1970), 211. For an extended discussion of a particular bourgeois notion, that of the artist, see ibid. 102 ff.
2. Cf. B. Thorne and N. Henley (eds.), *Language and Sex: difference and dominance* (Rowley, Mass. 1975) and R. Lakoff, 'Language and woman's place', *Language in Society*, 2 (1973), 45–80.
3. C. Belsey, *Critical Practice* (London 1980), 42.
4. Cf. R. Barthes, *Système de la mode* (Paris 1967), 265.
5. C. Belsey, op.cit. 47 ff. (She follows J. Williamson, *Decoding Advertisements* (London 1978).)
6. Ibid. 47.
7. Ibid. 49.
8. R. Barthes, *Mythologies* (Paris 1970), 173. 'To show the universality of human actions in the daily life of all the countries of the world: birth, death, work, knowledge, play, always impose the same types of behaviour; there is a family of man'. (Barthes, *Mythologies*, trans. Annette Lavers, London 1972, 100.)
9. Ibid. 'An ambiguous myth of the human "community" which serves as an alibi to a large part of our humanism.' (Trans. Lavers, op.cit. 100.)
10. Ibid. 174. 'Man is born, works, laughs and dies everywhere in the same way' (trans. A. Lavers, op.cit. 100); 'which we shall here quite simply call "injustice" ' (ibid. 101).
11. Ibid. 175. 'Whether or not the child is born with ease or difficulty, whether or not his birth caused suffering to his mother, whether or not he is threatened by a high mortality rate, whether or not such and such a type of future is open to him: this is what your Exhibition should be telling people, instead of an eternal lyricism of birth.' (Trans. A. Lavers, op.cit. 102.)
12. P. Thody, *Roland Barthes : a conservative estimate* (London 1977), 42.
13. Cf. I. A. Richards, *Practical Criticism* (1929, reprinted, London 1964), 53 ff.
14. J. Fiske and J. Hartley, *Reading Television* (London 1978), *passim*, esp. 116 ff. and 124 ff., 190 f.
15. Ibid. 41 ff. Further references in the text.

6.3 Marxism and the Dominant Ideology

1. R. Barthes, *Le Plaisir du texte* (Paris 1973), 53. 'There are those who want a text (an art, a painting) without a shadow, without the "dominant ideology"; but this is to want a text without fecundity, without productivity, a sterile text (see the myth of Woman without a Shadow). The text needs its shadow: this shadow is *a bit* of ideology, *a bit* of representation, *a bit* of subject: ghosts, pockets, traces, necessary clouds : subversion must produce its own chiaroscuro. (Commonly said : "dominant ideology". This expression is incongruous. For what is ideology? It is precisely the idea *insofar as it dominates*: ideology can only be dominant.') (Barthes, *The Pleasure of the Text*, trans. R. Miller, London 1976, 32.)
2. Cf. J. L. Sammons, *Literary Sociology and Practical Criticism* (Bloomington and London 1977), 60, whom I follow; but many similar accounts abound, cf. e.g. R. Williams, *Marxism and Literature* (Oxford 1977), 13 ff., and C. Slaughter, *Marxism, Ideology and Literature* (London 1980), 81 f., 187.
3. On Marx's view of Romanticism as an 'historically justified illusion' cf. C.

Slaughter, op.cit. 9, and F. Jameson, *The Political Unconscious* (London 1981), 96, pointing out that Romanticism was an 'ambiguous moment' in the resistance to capitalism. Of course all such generalizations have a certain fatuity. On the historically changing political positions of English romantics, cf. e.g. M. Butler, *Romantics, Rebels and Reactionaries* (Oxford 1981), *passim*.

4. Cf. L. Trotsky, *Literature and Revolution* (Ann Arbor 1960), 242 f.
5. Cf. K. Marx and F. Engels, *The German Ideology* (London 1967), 64 f.
6. Cf. J. L. Sammons, op.cit. 60.
7. R. Geuss thus summarizes Lukács's argument in *The Idea of a Critical Theory* (Cambridge 1981), 24, referring to G. Lukács, *Geschichte und Klassenbewusstsein* Neuwied and Berlin 1968), 87, 141, 148 ff., 357 ff.
8. The way in which the text reflects or expresses the dominant ideology is much discussed by Marxists: cf. e.g. T. Eagleton, *Criticism and Ideology* (London 1976), Ch.3 64–101, and C. Slaughter, op.cit., Chs.4–6.
9. G. Lukács, *The Historical Novel* (Harmondsworth 1969), 96 f.
10. C. Slaughter, op.cit. 129.
11. J. Bennett, *Formalism and Marxism* (London 1977), 39.
12. G. Lukács, in D. Craig, (ed.), *Marxists on Literature* (Harmondsworth 1975), 285.
13. Ibid.
14. Ibid. 287.
15. Ibid. 323.
16. Ibid. 288 f.
17. Ibid. 294; cf. 305.
18. Ibid. 303.
19. Ibid. 324.
20. Ibid. 334.
21. Ibid. 344.
22. Ibid. 348.
23. F. Jameson, op.cit. 20.
24. T. Eagleton, op.cit. 16.
25. P. Macherey, *Pour une théorie de la production littéraire* (Paris 1966), 66. 'For the purposes of theoretical analysis, the work is construed as a *centre* of interest although this does not imply that the work itself is *centred*.' (Macherey, *A Theory of Literary Production*, trans. G. Wall, London 1978, 52.)
26. Ibid. 103. 'The conflict of several meanings [which is not] resolved or absorbed, but simply *displayed*.' (Trans. G. Wall, op.cit. 84.)
27. Ibid. 113. Cf. T. Eagleton's discussion of the relation of Macherey to Freud, op.cit. 90 ff. 'The unconscious of the work (not of the author) . . . what we are seeking is analogous to that relationship which Marx acknowledges when he insists on seeing material relations as being derived from the social infrastructure behind all ideological phenomena . . . whence the possibility of reducing the ideological to the economic'. (Trans. G. Wall, op.cit. 92 f.)
28. P. Macherey, op.cit. 190. Further references in the text.
29. C. Belsey, *Critical Practice* (London 1980), 108.
30. T. Bennett, op.cit. 25.
31. C. Belsey, op.cit. 109, Cf. F. Jameson, op.cit. 48 ff.
32. P. Widdowson, Paul Stigant, and Peter Brooker, ' History and literary value', *Literature and History V*, 1 (1979), 2 ff. Further references in text.
33. I. Watt, *The Rise of the Novel* (Harmondsworth 1963), 62 ff.

6.4 The Moral and the Political

1. F. Jameson, *The Political Unconscious* (London 1981), 34.
2. T. Eagleton, *Criticism and Ideology* (London 1976), 176.
3. Cf. C. Butler in H. Schiff (ed.), *Contemporary Approaches to English Studies* (London 1977), 'Tragedy and Moral Education'.
4. W. Frankena, *Ethics* (Englewood Cliffs 1963), 4.
5. Ibid. 7 f.
6. Though Iris Murdoch has some severe criticisms to make of such philosopher's notions of the human agent in her *The Sovereignty of Good* (London 1970), 4 ff.
7. Some of the issues I shall raise are implicitly discussed from the point of view of Rawls's analysis of justice, by Michael J. Sandel, *Liberalism and the Limits of Justice* (Cambridge 1982).
8. The citations come from M. J. La Hood (ed.), *Tender is the Night : Essays in Criticism* (Bloomington and London 1969). Page references follow in the text. Since I have taken them from the most part out of context, I have not attributed them, except in one more extended case.
9. e.g. F. R. Leavis, *The Great Tradition* (Harmondsworth 1962), G. Steiner, *Tolstoy or Dostoevsky* (Harmondsworth 1967), J. Bayley, *The Characters of Love* (London 1968), P. Swinden, *Unofficial Selves* (London 1973), R. Langbaum, *Mysteries of Identity* (New York 1977).
10. W. J. Harvey, *Character and the Novel* (London 1965), 31, 71.
11. Cf. ibid. 155 ff.
12. Ibid. 26.
13. Ibid. 78, cf. 24. Harvey points out that such respect is significantly lacking in Madame Merle and Gilbert Osmond, ibid. 47 ff.
14. T. Eagleton, op.cit. 110 ff. Further references are in the text.
15. C. Belsey, in P. Widdowson (ed.), *Re-Reading English* (London 1982), 130.
16. Ibid. For a perhaps more direct and illuminating contrast of such historical frameworks, one might prefer to read John Fowle's *The French Lieutenant's Woman* (London 1969).
17. T. Eagleton op.cit. 43.
18. R. Williams, *Marxism and Literature* (Oxford 1977), 12.
19. And indeed of the individual creative writer; cf. Williams's discussion of this topic in ibid. 192 ff.
20. R. Coward and J. Ellis, *Language and Materialism* (London 1977), 1 f.
21. Ibid. 2
22. Including Coward and Ellis, op.cit., *passim*, esp. Ch.5, 61 ff. and Ch.6, 93 ff.; also C. Belsey, *Critical Practice* (London 1980), 64 ff., and Jameson, op.cit. 152 ff., all appealing to Lacan.
23. Cf. J. Derrida, 'Differance' in *Speech and Phenomena and other essays* translated by D. B. Allison (Evanston 1973), 145 f. His later work, notably *La Carte postale* (Paris 1980) suggests to me that Derrida is now more preoccupied with existentialist themes of responsibility for one's life and what one says about it.
24. Cf. Belsey, op.cit. 66, 86 ff., 122 ff.
25. B. Sharratt, *Reading Relations* (Brighton 1982), 154.
26. e.g. the worker may think that he 'freely' offers his labour in a capitalist market: cf. L. Althusser, *Lenin and Philosophy and other essays* (London 1971), 169.
27. F. Jameson, op.cit. 243. Further reference in the text.
28. Cf. Jameson's premiss, op.cit. that 'this book will argue from the priority of the political interpretation of literary texts' (17), 'Marxism subsumes other

interpretative modes or systems' (47). Of course any wholly explanatory ideology will attempt to do this—but we have argued that no such holistic system of belief is possible.

29. Conrad, *Lord Jim* (1900: reprinted Harmondsworth 1961), 16. Further references in the text.
30. This is Eagleton's phrase: op.cit. 138.
31. Cf. D. Forgacs on Goldmann's conception of the mental structure of the group, in A. Jefferson and D. Robey (eds.), *Modern Literary Theory* (London 1982), 152 ff.
32. T. Eagleton, op.cit. 134. Eagleton and Jameson of course presuppose the notion of the spontaneously incorporative nature of the dominant ideology.
33. Cf. Jameson, op.cit. 162 ff.
34. Cf. A. J. Guerard's application of the notions of 'sympathy and judgement' to *Lord Jim* in his *Conrad the Novelist* (Cambridge, Mass. 1958), 152–74.
35. Cf. E. Kamenka, *Marxism and Ethics* (London 1969), 35, 45.
36. Cf. ibid. 21, 22, 26. Kamenka also argues that Marx's notion of alienation as supersedable must be wrong, ibid. 27 ff., 42.
37. F. Jameson, op.cit. 60.
38. I. Berlin, *Four Essays on Liberty* (Oxford 1969), esp. that on 'Historical Inevitability', and cf. ibid. 47, 54, 63 f., 70 f.
39. This is, one supposes, Jameson's leap. The (moral) dangers of this position are eloquently expressed by Berlin, op.cit. 77.
40. C. Slaughter, *Marxism Ideology and Literature* (London 1980), 21, cf. 24. He goes on to argue that Lukács, Adorno, and Goldmann fail to do this.
41. Cf. J. Culler, *On Deconstruction* (London 1983), 43–63, with references.
42. This is the subtitle of P. Gay, *The Enlightenment: an Interpretation*, Vol.I (London 1967).
43. J. Bennett, *Formalism and Marxism* (London 1979), 11, 15.
44. K. Millett, *Sexual Politics* (London 1972), *passim*, and esp. 237–93.

BIBLIOGRAPHY

Bann, S., and Bowlt, S. (eds.) *Russian Formalism* (Edinburgh 1973).

Barnes, Barry *T. S. Kuhn and Social Science* (London 1982).

Barthes, Roland *Critical Essays* (New York 1972). *Mythologies* (Paris 1970). *Le Plaisir du texte* (Paris 1973). *S/Z* (Paris 1970). *Système de la mode* (Paris 1967).

Belsey, Catherine *Critical Practice* (London 1980).

Bennett, Tony *Formalism and Marxism* (London 1979).

Berlin, Isaiah *Essays on Liberty* (Oxford 1969).

Black, Max *Models and Metaphors* (Cornell 1962).

Bleich, David *Subjective Criticism* (Baltimore and London 1978).

Bloom, Harold, *et al. Deconstruction and Criticism* (London 1979).

Brooke-Rose, C. *A Grammar of Metaphor* (London 1958).

Butler, Christopher *After the Wake* (Oxford 1980).

Butler, Marilyn *Romantics, Rebels and Reactionaries* (Oxford 1971).

Cassirer, Ernst *An Essay on Man* (New Haven 1962).

Chatman, S. (ed.) *Literary Style* (New York 1971).

Ching, M. K. L., Haley, M. C. and Lunsford, R. F. (eds.) *Linguistic Perspectives on Literature* (London 1980).

Coward, Rosalind, and Ellis, John *Language and Materialism* (London 1977).

Craig, David (ed.) *Marxism and Literature* (Harmondsworth 1975).

Culler, Jonathan *On Deconstruction* (London 1983). *The Pursuit of Signs* (London 1981). *Structuralist Poetics* (London 1975).

Danto, A. C. *Analytical Philosophy of History* (Cambridge 1965).

de Beaugrande, R. *Text Discourse and Process* (London 1980).

de Man, Paul *Allegories of Reading* (New Haven 1979).

Derrida, Jacques *La Dissémination* (Paris 1972). *L'Écriture et la différence* (Paris 1967). *De la grammatologie* (Paris 1967). *Marges de la philosophie* (Paris 1972). *Positions* (Paris 1972).

Eagleton, Terry *Criticism and Ideology* (London 1976).

Eaton, T. (ed.) *Essays in Literary Semantics* (Heidelberg 1978).

Eco, Umberto *The Role of the Reader* (London 1981).

Erlich, Victor *Russian Formalism, History, Doctrine* (The Hague 1955).

Fischer, Ernst *Art Against Ideology* (London 1969).

Fiske, J., and Hartley, J. *Reading TV* (London 1978).

Fowler, Roger *Linguistics and the Novel* (London 1977). *Literature as Social Discourse* (London 1981).

Frankena, William *Ethics* (Englewood Cliffs 1963).

Freeman, D. C. (ed.) *Linguistics and Literary Style* (London 1970).

Gauthier, D. P. *Practical Reasoning* (Oxford 1963).

Genette, Gérard *Narrative Discourse* (Oxford 1980).

Geuss, R. *The Idea of a Critical Theory : Habermas and the Frankfurt School* (Cambridge 1981).

Goldman, Lucien *The Hidden God* (London 1964).
Goodman, Nelson *Ways of Worldmaking* (Indianapolis 1978).
Graff, Gerald *Literature Against Itself* (Chicago 1979).
Halliday, M. A. K. *Language as Social Semiotic* (London 1978).
——and A. McIntosh and P. Strevens *Linguistics and Language Teaching* (London 1964).
——and McIntosh, A. *Patterns of Language* (London 1966).
Harari, Josué V. (ed.) *Textual Strategies* (London 1980).
Hartman, Geoffrey *Criticism in the Wilderness* (New Haven 1980). *Saving the Text* (Baltimore and London 1981).
Harvey, W. J. *Character and the Novel* (London 1965).
Hawkes, Terence *Structuralism and Semiotics* (London 1977).
Heath, S. (ed.) *Roland Barthes: Image–Music–Text* (London 1977).
Henle, P. (ed.) *Language Thought and Culture* (Ann Arbor 1965).
Hirsch, E. D. *Aims of Interpretation* (Chicago 1976). *Validity in Interpretation* (New Haven 1967).
Holland, Norman H. *The Dynamics of Literary Response* (New York 1968).
Hoy, D. C. *The Critical Circle* (Berkeley and Los Angelos 1978).
Iser, Wolfgang *The Act of Reading* (Baltimore 1978).
Jakobson, Roman *Questions de poétique* (Paris 1973).
Jameson, Frederic *The Political Unconscious* (London 1981). *The Prison House of Language* (Princeton 1972).
Jefferson, A. and Robey, D. (eds.) *Modern Literary Theory* (London 1982).
Johnson, Barbara *The Critical Difference* (Baltimore 1980).
Kamenka, E. *Marxism and Ethics* (London 1969).
La Hood, Marvin J. (ed.) *Tender is the Night : Essays in Criticism* (Bloomington and London 1969).
Lakoff, George, and Johnson, Mark *Metaphors we Live by* (Chicago 1980).
Leech, G. N. *A Linguistic Guide to English Poetry* (London 1969). *Towards a Semantic Description of English* (London 1969).
Lentricchia, Frank *After the New Criticism* (London 1980).
Levin, Harry *The Gates of Horn* (New York 1966).
Lodge, David *The Modes of Modern Writing* (London 1977).
Lukács, Georg *The Historical Novel* (Harmondsworth 1969).
Macherey, Pierre *Pour une théorie de la production littéraire* (Paris 1966).
Macksey, R. and Donato E. (eds.) *The Structuralist Controversy* (Baltimore 1972).
Millett, Kate *Sexual Politics* (London 1972).
Murdoch, Iris *The Sovereignty of Good* (London 1970).
Norris, C. *Deconstruction* (London 1982).
Nowottny, W. *The Language Poets Use* (London 1962).
Ortony, Andrew (ed.) *Metaphor and Thought* (Cambridge 1979).
Pettit, Philip *The Concept of Structuralism* (Berkeley 1977).
Pitcher, George *The Philosophy of Wittgenstein* (Englewood Cliffs 1964).
Pratt, M.-L. *Towards a Speech Act Theory of Literary Discourse* (Bloomington and London 1977).
Richards, I. A. *Practical Criticism* (1929; reprinted London 1964).
Ricœur, Paul *La Métaphore vive* (Paris 1975).

Riffaterre, M. *Semiotics of Poetry* (London 1980).
Robbe-Grillet, Alain *Pour un nouveau roman* (Paris 1963).
Rorty, Richard *Consequences of Pragmatism* (Brighton 1982). *Philosophy and the Mirror of Nature* (Oxford 1980).
Sacks, S. (ed.) *On Metaphor* (Chicago 1979).
Sammons, J. L. *Literary Sociology and Practical Criticism* (Bloomington and London 1977).
Sandel, Michael J. *Liberalism and the Limits of Justice* (Cambridge 1982).
Sartre, J.-P. *What is Literature?* (London 1950).
Schiff, Hilda (ed.) *Contemporary Approaches to English Studies* (London 1977).
Scholes, Robert *Fabulation and Metafiction* (Chicago and London 1979). *Semiotics and Interpretation* (New Haven 1982).
Searle, John *Speech Acts* (Cambridge 1969).
Sebeok, T. A. (ed.) *Style in Language* (Boston 1960).
Sharratt, Bernard *Reading Relations* (Brighton 1982).
Slaughter, Cliff *Marxism Ideology and Literature* (London 1980).
Smith, N. and Wilson, D. *Modern Linguistics: the results of Chomsky's Revolution* (Harmondsworth 1977).
Sturrock, John (ed.) *Structuralism and Since* (Oxford 1979).
Thody, Philip *Roland Barthes: a conservative estimate* (London 1977).
Todorov, T. *Introduction à la littérature fantastique* (Paris 1970). *Poétique* (Paris 1967).
Trotsky, L. *Literature and Revolution* (Ann Arbor 1960).
Ullman, S. *Language and Style* (Oxford 1964). *Semantics* (Oxford 1962).
van Dijk, T. *Text and Context* (London 1971).
Watson, George *The English Ideology* (London 1973).
Watt, Ian *The Rise of the Novel* (Harmondsworth 1963).
Widdowson, Peter (ed.) *Re-Reading English* (London 1982).
Williams, Raymond *Marxism and Literature* (Oxford 1977).
Wittgenstein, L. *Philosophical Investigations* (Oxford 1953).
Young, Robert (ed.) *Untying the Text* (London 1981).

Index